S0-CEI-917

ALTERING THE "I"

We were a young Five, on our desert Trek seeking other Fives to form a city with. When these poor people came staggering across the desert at us shouting and waving their arms, we saw at once that they were all sick and out of their minds, because they weren't arranged in Fives.

They kept trying to join the Fives, and we prevented them; after all, they were stealing air, a horrid crime. Meanwhile the humans were madly trying to explain to us that all they wanted was water, water...

It was terribly funny; it was a splendid object lesson; and it was very nearly a disaster. It took me an hour to realize what I had done. We stopped the experiment promptly then, with explanations...

from the *Introduction*
by Ursula K. Le Guin

THE ALTERED I

EDITED BY LEE HARDING

A BERKLEY WINDHOVER BOOK
published by
BERKLEY PUBLISHING CORPORATION

Copyright © 1976, 1978 by Norstrilia Press

All rights reserved

Published by arrangement with Norstrilia Press, Lee Harding and
Ursula K. Le Guin, through the agency of Virginia Kidd

All rights reserved which includes the right
to reproduce this book or portions thereof in
any form whatsoever. For information address

Berkley Publishing Corporation
200 Madison Avenue
New York, New York 10016

SBN 425-03849-1

*BERKLEY WINDHOVER BOOKS are published by
Berkley Publishing Corporation
200 Madison Avenue
New York, N. Y. 10016*

BERKLEY WINDHOVER BOOK ® TM 106 2206

Printed in the United States of America

Berkley Windhover Edition, May, 1978

To Carey Handfield

The First Australian Science Fiction Writers'
Workshop, Booth Lodge, Kallista, Victoria,
August 1975.

Writer in Residence: Ursula K. Le Guin
Oregon, U.S.A.

Those attending:

Derrick Ashby *Victoria*
Bruce Barnes *Tasmania*
Kathryn Buckley *Queensland*
John Edward Clark *Queensland*
Barbara J. Coleman *Victoria*
Randal Flynn *Queensland*
Rob Gerrand *Victoria*
Bruce Gillespie *Victoria*
David Grigg *Victoria*
Graeme Lunn *Victoria*
Marian Maddern *Victoria*
Pip Maddern *Victoria*
Edward Mundie *Victoria*
Annis Shepherd *Victoria*
Petrina Smith *New South Wales*
Kitty Vigo *Victoria*
Stefan Vucak *Victoria*
Andrew Whitmore *Victoria*
Robert Young *South Australia*

Contents

Editor's Note

The twenty members of the workshop produced between them approximately ninety manuscripts, varying in length from 250 to 5,000 words. It was from this formidable mountain of typescript that I was asked to make a selection for this book.

But from the beginning I felt that something more substantial than a collection of stories was needed if we wanted to convey some idea of how the workshop functioned. I asked the members if they would mind writing some factual articles that would provide important background material, and they responded to my request with astonishing alacrity. I would like to thank every one of them for being so completely in accord throughout the long period of planning.

It was from this second and equally impressive set of contributions that I made my final selections to accompany the fiction. The sheer volume of manuscripts made it impossible for me to include as much as I would have liked, but I feel confident that a balanced book has been achieved. Except for simple copy editing, the stories appear here exactly as they were written during the workshop. Extensive revision of any of the mss. would have negated the major purpose of *The Altered I:* to demonstrate how creativity can be encouraged and fostered under special conditions.

This book would never have appeared had it not been for the vision and drive of a handful of people: Carey Handfield, of Norstrilia Press, whose dream it first was and to whom I am indebted for the privilege of editing it; David Grigg and Kitty Vigo who helped to organize people in the early stages; Ursula Le Guin, whose marvelous idea for the Transglobal workshopping of her story fired my imagination, nudged the book into its final shape and supplied us with a title; Virginia Kidd, who acted so conscientiously on Ursula's behalf; and Rob Gerrand, who as well as providing wise counsel and encouragement all along, stepped in and helped mightily during the final stages of putting the book together.

LEE HARDING
Melbourne, 1976

Bruce Gillespie

Foreword

The period of organizing the workshop was the most crowded nine months of my life.

The workshop was Ursula Le Guin's idea—indeed, her pet project—from the beginning. The Committee for the 33rd World Science Fiction Convention (Aussiecon, held in Melbourne during mid-August, 1975) had already chosen Ursula Le Guin as its Guest of Honor. This choice was understandable. Her science fiction novels, including *The Left Hand of Darkness,* are among the very best in the field. For my taste her trilogy of Earthsea novels are *the* best in the fantasy field. The knowledge that Ursula Le Guin would be our Guest of Honor was a continuing source of elation; at the peak of her career, she would be visiting *us.*

But Guests of Honor, it seems, are not people to stand on pedestals at science fiction conventions. In late 1974, Ursula Le Guin made it plain that, while she would be in Australia, she wanted to advance some project that would have lasting benefit for the Australian science fiction world. The project which she suggested was a workshop for aspiring and previously unpublished writers of science fiction.

Ursula had already been a writer-in-residence at Clarion Writers' Workshops and similar events in the USA. During the last ten years, these workshops have become famous for their intense, hard-working approach to developing the talents of would-be writers—and for the number of now-practicing science-fiction writers who have begun their careers there. However, no workshop of this kind had yet been conducted in Australia. Any such project would need to be based upon the detailed advice from Ursula herself,

1

and put into effect by an Administrative Organizer in Australia.

Robin Johnson was Chairman of the 33rd World SF Convention, and had quite enough worries by December 1974 without trying to organize a writers' workshop as well. He had to appoint an Administrative Organizer in a hurry; he said to me, "You're It."

In December 1974, long before the workshop itself was due to be held, the main problem confronting the Committee was raising enough money to hold the workshop at all. Also, we wanted the workshop to fit two main criteria:

(1) The attendees should be as physically comfortable as possible, so that they would have maximum time and opportunity to concentrate on writing and discussion. For instance, we had to bear in mind that the workshop would be held in the middle of a Melbourne winter.
(2) The organization of the workshop program should follow, as far as possible, the specifications suggested by Ursula Le Guin.

Robin Johnson and I made an application for funds to the Literature Board of the Australia Council. In March 1975, the Board made a substantial grant toward the running of the workshop itself, and toward travel expenses for Ursula Le Guin's journey to Australia. In June 1975, the Board made a much-needed grant toward the traveling and accommodation expenses of those people who wished to attend the workshop. Now we had the funds—but how to make sure it would be a success?

This foreword is mainly a catalogue of the people who helped me to do my job—in fact, those who did most of it for me. For instance, in February 1975, the long-suffering Carey Handfield could be seen driving me around hairpin bends and down rough bush tracks in the Dandenong Ranges in search of a suitable site for the workshop. The Melbourne Tourist Bureau provided our most promising lead. They suggested Booth Lodge, about two miles beyond Belgrave. Carey and I drove there, talked to the staff for half an hour, and decided that nothing should stop us from making Booth Lodge the site for the workshop. The facilities include a very large house, containing meeting halls, a dining room, a kitchen, and a self-contained flat, and recently built sleeping quarters. Each block had room for eleven people, plus a central common room. Situated in an isolated area of the Dandenong Ranges, about thirty miles from the center of Melbourne, surrounded by trees, its placid, uninterrupted working atmosphere made it the right place for our requirements.

After those site-finding expeditions, most of the preparations for the workshop were fairly routine, but posed some unique problems. How, for instance, could I let young writers throughout Australia know that the workshop was being held? I'm not sure that I solved the answer to this problem. A number of people who would have liked to attend the workshop did not hear about it until too late. I tried various methods of publicity, including a news sheet released to the press and media, information distributed through the various state branches of the Fellowship of Australian Writers (perhaps our most valuable source of publicity) and, of course, information in the *Progress Report* of the World Convention itself.

I received 46 inquiries for application forms: 29 from Victoria, 6 from New South Wales, 4 from Queensland, 2 from Western Australia, 2 from Tasmania, 1 from ACT, 1 from South Australia, and 1 from New Zealand. Each person was required to submit at least one short story at least 5000 words long with his or her application form. Eventually 23 people from 4 states submitted stories, and 19 were accepted to attend the workshop (1 person dropped out on the first day, so that there were 20 attending altogether, including Ursula and me).

These figures are deceptive. They hide a long process of receiving bits of paper, posting letters, sending great bundles of manuscripts by airmail to Ursula, and making friends with several prospective attendees who took the trouble to phone me. Ursula kept sending back enthusiastic letters and enjoining me to "keep up my courage" until August. From May until July, we sorted out the innumerable fine details that were needed to weave the web of a functioning community of 20 for a week.

A central task involved in running the workshop was the photocopying. Ursula had asked that each member should be able to read the stories submitted by every other member, both at the beginning of the workshop and as people wrote new work during the week itself. The initial task of photocopying included 20 copies of each 19 stories. The entire job was taken over by Ken Ford, John Ham, and Don Ashby.

As we traveled by car convoy to Booth Lodge, after an evening meal at the rendezvous point, Cahill's Restaurant in Melbourne, I kept thinking to myself, "Will it go right? What can go wrong? How did I get *into* all this?"

And found that the members of the workshop not only made my job easy, but took it away from me altogether. When I arrived at Booth Lodge, everybody else was already gathered in a circle, quite silent, each person reading everybody else's manuscripts. The photocopying machine was ready for operation. Rooms had been chosen; typewriters unpacked. And, most reassuring of all, Mrs. Margery Chisholm, the administrator of Booth Lodge, was there to help me calm down and to make sure that everything ran smoothly.

Ursula Le Guin arrived on the Saturday morning after a hectic few days in Sydney, and at last I could shake hands with one of the people I admire most. After a very brief rest, she joined us in the main room, and we began the wearying, exhilarating, often hilarious task of workshopping stories, creating new ones, and re-creating ourselves.

The rest of this book tells the story of that week's experience. We were surrounded by an atmosphere of dripping trees, the incessant, comforting sound of typing, and the warmth of each other's company. My part in the experience is just a footnote; I was left with nothing to do! Within a day or so, the others had decided to do their own photocopying, arrange any extra provisions that were needed, and stick to time schedules. What did I do? I wrote stories of course. For the first time in four years, the encouragement from Ursula and the members of the workshop freed some blockage from my brain and I found myself typing stories at 3 A.M., just like everybody else.

The only way I can summarize such an experience is in the way I tried to say it to Ursula Le Guin herself: that she trusted us to trust each other to trust ourselves.

And I was there too.

Ursula K. Le Guin

Introduction

The usual scenario for a writer's conference or workshop, I am told by those who have been there, is something like this: The Writer sits on a dais facing a group of Postulant Writers. He criticizes the works which they have submitted to him, and lectures on the art of writing. In the evenings, he reads to them from his works.

The kind of workshop I seem to get involved in is not like that at all: it is incredibly messy. There are all these people, about twenty of them, sitting, or lying, or lounging, or assuming the lotus position, or whatever, in a sort of circle. Somewhere nearby are stacks of the manuscripts submitted for tomorrow; they have all already read the manuscripts submitted for today. They start in on the first story, and one by one, round the circle, they voice their criticisms and reactions: anything relevant, from grammar and structure through factual probability to the implicit Outlook on Life. The author of the story is not allowed to reply until they are all done; then he/she can reply passionately and at length. The professional writer, often called the "resident"—President without the capital P, perhaps—can either criticize in turn, or try to sum up at the end; she/he has no special authority, except to say, "Come on, Susan already said all that," when people begin repeating one another, and to open general discussion, and to prevent fist-fights. This round robin of discussion usually goes on from nine till noon, and again in the afternoon if there's a big backlog of stories to work on. The rest of the day and night, everybody writes—perhaps on a theme or exercise proposed by the resident, perhaps on their own hook—and reads what everybody else has written, and talks, and writes, and writes, and talks, and eats meals with the others, and occasionally, for brief periods in the small hours, even sleeps a little. This goes on, twenty hours a day, five or six days a week, for six weeks. Residents last only a week apiece, and are taken away to rest homes; fresh victims are supplied regularly.

This system of mutual criticism sessions was worked out at a conference of professional science-fiction writers at Milford, Pennsylvania (and Milford Conferences still take place annually both in the United States and England). A survivor of a "Milford," Professor Robin Scott Wilson, applied its egalitarian method to a workshop for aspiring sf writers at Clarion, Pennsylvania. The experiment was notably successful, and "Clarions" have been held annually at one or more places in the States each summer since then.

I have been a resident three times at the six-week Clarion West workshops organized by Vonda McIntyre at the University of Washington, and have also applied the system, so far as is possible, to once-a-week courses in the writing of sf and fantasy, twice with Professor Anthony Wolk in Oregon, and once at the University of Reading in England. When I needed to earn my way to Australia to attend the World Science Fiction Convention in Melbourne in August of '75, the Australian Literature Board generously provided the opportunity for a one-week "Clarion of the Antipodes." I leapt at the chance with delight, having found workshop residence as exciting as it is exhausting.

The excitement is twofold. Part of it is that, under these rather extreme conditions—twenty people living, eating, talking, and working together, in a situation of extreme ego-exposure, and with obsessive concentration on a single goal—a group forms: the kind of group, I take it, that encounter therapy sets out deliberately to form. Participation in a real group is always exciting for a writer, whose work is done in solitude (usually outer, always inner): a rare and invigorating experience. The other element of the excitement is the functioning of the system itself. The participants write; and they tend to write better as they go along. Stories written in the workshop, under pressure, often in a halfday or a night, are very often much better than the lovingly worked-on stories submitted ahead of time as evidence of qualification. This improvement must rise from the fact that the participants are getting practice in criticism and therefore in self-criticism—and a taste of the self-confidence that comes with self-criticism; and also I think they write better because they are caught up in and carried by the momentum and energy of the group. When the system works, as it usually does, it is not a competitive situation; just the reverse. It provides mutual inspiration.

This is the most commonplace thing in the world to a performing musician, whose art is a group performance, and who depends upon that mutual release of energy through skill. To a writer, it can be a revelation. "The competition," to a young fiction-writer, usually consists of famous or successful authors, none of whom he knows personally, and most of whom are dead: a remote untouchable crowd of luminaries. To meet, live with, work with, a group of ambitious, serious, non-famous, not-yet-successful writers like one's self, to find that you aren't the only nut on the walnut tree, to discuss the craft, to argue ideas, to expose your work to others as they expose it to you, no holds barred, is to experience what the musician experiences and relies upon in every performance: cooperation on the job, skill reinforcing skill, not competition but emulation.... And music is made. Stories are written.

The American Clarions have produced a remarkable percentage of participants who go on to become professional writers. This is something to be proud of. But it's not the real point, I think. The real point is to make music together.

I should like to describe the music we made at Booth Lodge in the Dandenong Ranges, but it's always hard to put tunes into words. Some bits and fragments will have to do.

Before I ever came to Australia, the workshop had in a sense begun. In the early summer, Bruce Gillespie had sent airmail to Oregon (to the joy of the Australian Postal Commission) two fat packets of manuscript—the aspirant-workshoppers' stories. Our first job was to pick out and eliminate any obviously unready candidates (there were very few). Then (to the joy of the U.S. Post Office) I airmailed it all back. When I got to Sydney, all the manuscripts of the twenty accepted candidates were there ready for me to re-read in the few days before the workshop began. I did so, in what few spare moments the friendly Sydney science-fiction people left me, with crossed eyes. Sometimes all the stories seemed remarkable, sometimes they all seemed remarkably ghastly. Obviously I was going to be totally incompetent at this workshop. Oh why had I offered to do it, and what was I doing here where even Orion is cross-eyed?

The Lodge is a lovely place for a workshop, isolated from all distractions in those beautiful hills, nothing to lead the mind astray except perhaps a passing kookaburra. I wrote in my notebook on the second night, "This incredible Oregon-green mist-veiled rainy cold sweet silent birdsinging place..." I was still thoroughly jet-lagged, waking up at five every morning and wilting like a radish by seven at night, and had been living mostly on Lomotil for a week. I was driven out with Robin Johnson from Melbourne, midmorning on a coldish late-winter Saturday of August. The manageress of the Lodge, Mrs. Chisholm, the soul of kindness, brought me a cup of tea, and Bruce Gillespie, the organizer and Coordinator of the workshop—a horrible, thankless, endless job of keeping everybody fed and housed, copying everybody's stories, maintaining everybody's sanity, etc., etc.—made me welcome. And then they hurled me into this room where nineteen people were sitting alertly, like lions in the Coliseum, looking interested, but hungry.

They were so keen to start that they'd already started. I hastily explained the System, and everybody said who they were, and off we went. There has to be a first victim. I picked one because he looked resilient. He turned out to be Randal, the youngest participant. Infant sacrifice. But fortunately, he *was* resilient.

We began with the stories they had submitted when applying to join the workshop. An uneven lot of stories, one compared to another and also within themselves—lots of good stuff, bogs of imitation, sloughs of despond, lightning flashes of brilliance, great ideas badly worked out, stale ideas beautifully imagined, stories with no ending, stories with adipose middles, stories that were all beginning. Plenty to criticize, both negatively and positively. Plenty of work to do together. And they did it. Oh boy, did they do it!

Of the groups I have worked with, the Australians were the most serious, the least willing to waste time, and the—I don't know what word to use—the most good-natured, the gentlest? Not that they cautiously watered down their criticism, or played any I'll-praise-your-story-and-you-praise-mine games; they were too intent on writing to wander off into those dead ends. But they seemed to be instinctively aware of what it takes to make a group work as a group: There must be no bosses, and no cliques; during criticism sessions merely personal comments must be repressed; there must be no

Scapegoat, no Hero, and no shy Person-in-the-corner who doesn't participate. They avoided all these dangers. Their tact and skill was extraordinary, particularly when you consider that these were twenty people between seventeen and forty-five, almost all strangers to one another, with nothing evidently in common but the desire to write well. Of course, it was fantasy and science fiction they wanted to write; that did form the bond of mutual lunacy. And also, they were good. The quantity, and the wild variety, of talent and imagination waiting to break loose there was extraordinary. There wasn't a dud in the box.

It was I that endangered the harmony, by one stupid experiment, the contemplation of which has edified me ever since. Along about Tuesday, after three or four days, which in a workshop equals about six months of Real Time, when we all knew each other better than we had ever known our next of kin, and everybody was turning out reams of insane prose at a velocity approaching the speed of light, we fell to discussing one of the central areas of science fiction—the Alien, and the Human-Alien Relation. I was moaning about the way many sf writers skip blithely over the problems of alienness, just tacking a few tentacles or queer mating habits onto a standard Anglo-Saxon Cardboard Man and calling it a Pxzquilchian Native. When we get culture-shock just from visiting a different human society, what will it be like to meet a real alien? Will we even recognize truly alien intelligence when we meet it—have we already failed to do so, in the Cetacea? The question of communication is infinitely complex and stimulating, and instead of glossing it over with "translating machines" sf writers might face it, and draw strength from that very complexity, as Lem did in *Solaris*. And so on. And Kitty said, we ought to do an object-lesson in that . . . I jumped at the idea. Within ten minutes I had divided us up into Aliens and Humans. I was an Alien, of course; that was why I wanted to do it—playacting.

The five Aliens went off to my room for an hour and madly constructed their society, culture, and language. Then, after dinner, the Humans crashlanded on our desert planet (the big conference room of Booth Lodge). All they had to do was communicate with us in the most basic terms: We need help. We need water, shelter, food. We come from very far away.

The Aliens were untentacled and fully humanoid in looks; they even spoke Pidgin Galactic. The communication problems rose from the peculiarities of the Alien physiology and culture. The Aliens actually consisted of two symbiotic species, one bearded, which breathed in oxygen and exhaled carbon dioxide, the other beardless, which breathed in CO_2 and exhaled O. Two beards and three Beardless made a Five, a symbiotic unit. If you lost part of your Five and couldn't find replacements, your Five was Broken and had no chance of survival—you suffocated, in fact. A Five mated with another Five; a Ten was a married couple; Ten Tens was a City, the basic cultural unit. We were a Young Five, on our desert trek seeking other Fives to form a City with. Each member of the Five was only partly independent of the others psychologically, and would ask the other four things like, "Am I frightened? Do I approve?"—"I" being the Five, not the individual. When we did not understand something we observed coldly in unison, "I do not breathe your air." Well, so when these poor people came staggering across the desert at us shouting and waving their arms, we saw at once that they were all sick and out of their minds, because they weren't arranged in Fives. We hastened to arrange them properly, three Beardless and two Beards, all leaning close together and breathing hard at each other to restore the brain-cells. There was a curious shortage of Beards, so we could only make two proper Fives; the rest were Broken, and we sadly abandoned them to their fate. They kept trying to join the Fives, and we prevented them; after all, they were stealing air, a horrid crime. Meanwhile, the Humans were madly trying to explain to us that all they wanted was water, water, drink, drink and getting excited and breaking loose from their Fives, at which we were deeply distressed and pushed their heads back together, because what good is water if you can't breathe? . . .

It was terribly funny; it was a splendid object-lesson; and it was very nearly a disaster.

After all, it was really funny only to us, the Aliens—because only we knew what was going on. We had formed an ingroup, deliberately excluding the others, deliberately frustrating them, deliberately refusing to communicate.

Human tempers got short. For the first time when the group was all together, people wrangled and snarled at each other, withdrew, got sulky or bossy. People tried to take charge and coordinate the communications effort, but somebody else always had a better idea and shouted louder.

It took me an hour to realize what I had done. We stopped the experiment promptly then, with explanations. Everybody went off to their rooms very soon after. It was the only time that I saw the group really shaken. Next morning all was well. But Communications with Aliens was not a favorite subject after that.

The Grongs, however, remained with us all week. The Grongs must have come up on Sunday; my recollection is that somebody remarked incredulously that on his way to the workshop he had passed through a town named Grong Grong. And somebody else said of course, that's where the Grongs live. And somebody else said, what *do* Grongs use wattle for, actually? And from then on there was no controlling it. The mysterious reproductive ritual of the Grongs, which involves singing over the cabbages at night, was discovered. It was established that auctioneers shout Growing, Growing, Grong, and that two grongs do not make a gright; the resident made unappreciated references to that dolphin-torn, that grong-tormented sea; and so on. And on, and on. Workshopping is a tension-making business. You get awfully silly in the off moments. By Thursday, when anybody mentioned grongs everybody else screamed in unison.

Because this was only a week's session, with little time for writing full-scale stories, I used more exercises than I would in a six-week session. Most of my exercises are stolen from other people's workshops—I hear about them from the participants, and when they say, "That one really worked," I steal it. Our first one was the One-Change Bit. You take the world, and you change one thing in it, one little fact or condition, physical or social, just one; then you tell your story without ever saying what the change is—*showing* it in the behavior of the characters, the look of the scenery, or whatever. The purpose of this of course is practice in indirect explication, the conveyance of information without a lecture, an abstract disquisition, an Expository Lump; a necessary skill to any story-teller, and especially important in science fiction and fantasy. It is also a lesson in Ecology, since you find that one small change can have the most enormous secondary effects; everything is interwoven. Several people took this as a challenge to the reader's ingenuity and wrote a puzzle-story, but there were some beautiful leaps of the imagination made at the roaring typewriters that night.

Next day we had the Avram Davidson Word Game (I stole it from Avram Davidson; if he stole it, never mind.) The resident makes up two lists—mine was twenty adjectives and twenty nouns, this time; you can do it with all nouns, too—and cuts them into slips, and each participant draws two, blind. So you arrive at enigmatic combinations such as Pensive Fig, Traumatic Mittens, Unstable Ring, and all you have to do then is write a story with that title or theme. The purpose of this one is to prove you can write a story about anything, if you have to. And they did. Twenty beautiful stories. They were incredible. I suppose my favorite was Pip's; she made of her rather unpromising *Broken Pit* a ridiculous tale about a lot of hardworking and intransigently dunderheaded dwarves—I liked it because the dwarves were so much like us.

Next day, having decided that many of us were a bit weak on dialogue, and knowing that I have always been weak on dialogue, I decreed a Dialogue: without stage-directions or narrative: between a man and a woman in a spaceship about to make a forced landing. The two people had to be called merely A and B, and the reader was to be able to know, by the end, which was the man and which the woman. We read these aloud. Again there were a lot of beauties. Ted Mundie read A in mine so well that he nearly made me cry, which was unfair of him. Andrew Whitmore wrote a dialogue consisting almost entirely of one-sided silences. There was seldom much doubt which was the man and which the woman; but so many of them had had their couple quarrelling or quarrelsome that my next and final request was for a love story.

There aren't many love stories in science fiction. We did not make a great breakthrough. I should say that what we got was two Love stories and seventeen Lust stories. But after all, it had been a very hard week.

In the middle of the week, on Wednesday, we had all needed a break, and nine of us went for a hike in the Sherbrooke National Forest, just down the road. It was a soft rainy day. We passed a roadsign that said:

SLOW
LYREBIRDS
CROSS

This is my favorite roadsign in all the world. We heard a kookaburra, or perhaps a lyrebird imitating a kookaburra—you cannot be sure, they tell me; and perhaps I have got it backwards. We walked down the strange, sparse, dim, grand aisles of an Australian forest. We went down, and down, and down. Do Australian hills not have Up sides? Evidently not. We went on down. In the path before us lay a large, curiously segmented, green turd. There was a scratch from a strong triple claw in the earth beside it. All gathered round. Nine heads bent solemnly above the mystery. Wombat? Echidna? Grong? Nobody was sure. Later, there was another, also with the triple scratch beside it. We went on down.

When we finally rebelled and started up, we got lost. Wills and King had nothing on us for sheer mismanagement. We took about forty minutes to go about forty meters, in a weird woodlot-bramblepatch-cum-pot-holes we got into—a shortcut, of course. When we got out we went downhill again, defeated. We found a village called Selby and had a goody at the Milk Bar and called Booth Lodge, and noble persons with automobiles came and drove us home.

I wrote that night in my notebook, "Eucalyptus and tree ferns, wattle, broom, a tall white heather blooming. Wet, mist-showers, gleams of sun. Smells of mud and rain and eucalyptus. Bellbirds, kookaburra, unknown flutings and cries. O the strange birdsongs in the strange trees!"

Later, the next week, at the convention in Melbourne, Pip and Marian brought me a little hand-painted box full of gumtree leaves and wattle-flowers and all: Australian Smells, to take with me. It still works. Even in February in Golders Green, London NW 11, it works. Shut eyes, open box: I'm there. Down, down, down under.

And the whole lot of them came and abducted me at the convention and presented me with a tall golden Corinthian column, on top of which is a repulsively deformed Neanderthal type carrying a sign that says "You Love Me Only for My Body," and on the base of which is a plaque that says "Grong Award, 1975. To Ursula K. Le

Grong. For Singing Over the Cabbages." I have never and will never receive an award that gives me such undiluted pleasure. I'll pawn my Hugoes if I have to, but I will never part with my Grong.

We did make music. Some of it was very odd indeed, and most of it was tentative; but it was music. And the group, the mutuality, that formed: how rare, and how real, that was, may perhaps be seen in this book, which is the product of a year's cooperation by twenty strangers who spent a week together in the hills.

THE TRANSGLOBAL
WORKSHOP

When this volume began to be seriously discussed, it occurred to me that it might be both exemplary and entertaining to include in it a story actually written during a workshop, the extempore criticisms by the workshoppers, and the author's reply: thus reconstructing in print a typical workshop session. I felt, like any Noble Scientist experimenting with Deadly Germs, that I should volunteer as the first victim. After all, I have had time to build up some immunity to printed criticism, which is much more painful than the oral form. And anyhow, all the workshoppers' workshop stories had been discussed at Booth Lodge, while I had one they had never seen and thus could come at fresh, fangs bared, tentacles palpitating.

I wrote "The Eye Altering" during the workshop at Portland State University in the spring of 1975, and submitted it to that group. Their criticisms were interesting but perhaps too gentle, and only one or two pressed me hard on what I soon came to see as the major flaw in this version of the story.

It is not a first draft, since I write in longhand; it is what I call "first typed draft," which means that it has undergone spot revision in the process of being typed up but it's still pretty close to the original scrawl. Normally a story I submit for publication has been revised in typescript, and then either rewritten or revised-and-retyped at least once more entirely. When this story reappears in this anthology, it will have undergone all that—with the guidance, in this case, of my nineteen critics—an unusual boon!

It seems very much a "workshop story" to me in several ways: in that it was written all at a blow, without preliminary brooding or hatching, straight off under pressure; also, in that it was a direct response to workshop stimulus. A Portland State workshopper had written a story about allergy problems on an alien planet. It got heavily criticized, and the author confessed that he had been laid low with allergy symptoms all week and the story was his revenge, a sort of psychic antihistamine. But this subject intrigued me, fired me. Emulation occurred...

So here is our Experiment. First the story, written in Oregon; then a transcript of the taping of the workshoppers in Melbourne criticizing it; then the author's reply after listening to the tape in London. Ladies and gentlemen, the first Transglobal Workshop Session.

URSULA K. LE GUIN

Ursula K. Le Guin

The Eye Altering

Miriam stood at the big window of the infirmary ward and
looked out at the view and thought, For twenty-five years I have been
standing at this window and looking out at this view. And never once
have I seen what I wanted to see. Nor will I ever see it. Never again. O
Jerusalem, if I forget thee!

The sky above the flat, worn hills was gray. Southward, over the
low ridge called Ararat, the sun was setting; setting slowly, for New
Zion had a slower spin than Old Earth, and a twenty-eight hour day;
settling, rather than setting—settling slowly, dully, stupidly down
onto the dull, stupid horizon. No clouds picked up color from it to
end the long day in splendor. There were seldom any clouds. Only the
windless gray haze, sometimes thicker, sometimes thinner. When the
haze thickened it turned into rain, a fine, misty, smothering rain.
When it thinned, as now, it hung high and vague, formless. It never
quite cleared. You never saw the stars. You never saw the color of the
sky. And through the haze the sun—oh not the sun! not the sun, but
NSC 641 (Class G)—burned swollen and vaporous, warty as an
orange—remember oranges? the oranges of Haifa? the sweet juice on
the tongue?—a big, dull, bleary eye. Staring. You could always look
straight at NSC 641. It did not blind you with its glory. It stared down
and you stared up, with an idiot's unrecognizing stare.

Shadows stretched out across the valley toward the buildings of
the Settlement. In shadow the fields and woods were black; in the
light they were brown, purplish, and dirty red. Dirty colors, the colors
you got when you scrubbed your watercolors too much and the
teacher came by and said, You'd better use some fresh water, Mimi,
it's getting muddy. Because the teacher had been too kind to say to a

17

ten-year-old, That picture's a total loss, Mimi, throw it away and start fresh.

She had thought of that before—she had thought all her thoughts before, standing at this window—but this time it reminded her of Genya, because of the painting, and she turned to see how he was doing. The shock symptoms were almost gone, his face was no longer so pale and his pulse had steadied. While she held his wrist he sighed a bit and opened his eyes. Lovely eyes he had, gray in the thin face. He had never been much but eyes, poor Genya. Her oldest patient. Twenty-four years he had been her patient, right from the moment of his birth, five pounds, purplish-blue like a fetal rat, a month premature and half dead of cyanosis: the fifth child born on New Zion, the first in Ararat Settlement. A native. A very feeble and unpromising native. He hadn't even had the strength, or the sense, to cry at his first breath of this alien air. Sofia's other children had been full term and healthy, two girls, both married and mothers now, and fat Leon who could hoist a 150-pound sack of grain when he was fifteen. Good young colonists, strong stock. But Miriam had always loved Genya, and all the more after her own years of miscarriages and stillbirths, and the last birth, the girl who had lived two hours, whose eyes had been clear gray like Genya's. Babies never had gray eyes, the eyes of the newborn are blue, that was all sentimental rubbish. But how could you ever make sure of what color things were under this damned warty-orange sun? Nothing ever looked right. "So there you are, Gennady Borisovich," she said, "back home, eh?"

It had been their joke when he was a child; he had spent so much time in the infirmary that whenever he came in with one of his fevers or fainting spells or terrible belly-cramps he would say, "Here I am, back home, Auntie Doctor..."

"What happened?" he asked.

"You folded up; hoeing down in the South Field. Aaron and Tina brought you up here on the tractor. Touch of sunstroke, maybe? You've been doing all right, haven't you?"

He shrugged and smiled. "Fair."

"Cramps? Dizzy?"

"Sometimes."

"Why didn't you come to the clinic?"

"It's no good, Miriam."

Since he was grown he had called her Miriam. She missed "Auntie Doctor." He had grown away from her, these last three or four years: withdrawn. The withdrawal had begun when he took to painting so much. He had always sketched and painted, but now, all his free time and whatever energy he had left when his Settlement duties were done, he spent in the loft of the generator building where he'd made a kind of studio, grinding colors from rocks and mixing dyes from native plants, making brushes by begging pigtail-ends off little girls, and painting—painting on scrap from the lumber mill, on bits of rag, on precious scraps of paper, on smooth slabs of slate from the quarry on Ararat if nothing better was at hand. Painting portraits, scenes of Settlement life, buildings, machinery, still-lifes, plants, landscapes, inner visions. Painting anything, everything. His portraits had been much in demand—people were always kind to Genya and the other sicklies—but lately he had not done any portraits; he had gone in for abstracts, queer muddy jumbles of forms and lines all in a dark haze, like worlds half created. Nobody liked those paintings, but nobody ever told Genya he was wasting his time. He was a sickly; he was an artist; OK. Nobody who was healthy had time to be an artist. There was too much work to do. But it was good to have an artist. It was human. It was like Earth. Wasn't it?

They were kind to Toby, too, whose stomach troubles were so bad that at sixteen he weighed eighty-four pounds; kind to little Shura, who was just learning to talk at six, and whose eyes wept and wept all day long, even when she was smiling; kind to all their sicklies, the ones whose bodies could not adapt to this alien world, whose stomachs could not digest the native proteins even with the help of the "metas," the metabolizing pills which every colonist must take twice a day every day of his life on New Zion. Hard as life was in the Twenty Settlements, much as they needed every hand to work, they were gentle with their useless ones, their afflicted. In affliction the hand of God is visible. They remembered the words civilization, humanity. They remembered Jerusalem.

"Genya, my dear, what do you mean, it's no good?"

His quiet voice had frightened her. "It's no good," he had said, smiling. And the gray eyes not clear but veiled, hazy.

"Just that. It's no good. Medicine, cures, pills."

"Of course you know more about medicine than I do," Miriam

said. "You're a much better doctor than I am. Or are you giving up? Is that it, Genya? Giving up?" Anger had come on her so suddenly, from so deep within, from fear and despair so long and deeply hidden, that it shook her body and cracked her voice.

"I'm giving up one thing. The metas."

"The metas? Giving them up? What are you talking about?"

"I haven't taken any for two weeks."

The rage and terror swelled in her; she felt her face go crimson, heard her voice rough as a woodrasp—"Two weeks! And so, and so, and so you're here! Where do you think you'd end up, you terrible fool? Lucky you're not dead!"

"I haven't been any worse since I stopped taking them, Miriam. In fact maybe better, the last few days. Not good, but better. Until today. I think it was heatstroke. I ... forgot to wear a hat ..." Saying this he looked ashamed. It was stupid to go to work in the fields bareheaded; NSC 641 was capable, for all its dull look, of hitting the unsheltered human head quite as hard as fiery Sol, and Genya was apologetic for his carelessness. "You see, I was really feeling so well this morning, I kept right up with the others, hoeing. Then I felt a bit dizzy, but I didn't want to stop, it was so good to be able to work with the others, I never thought about heatstroke."

Miriam found that there were tears in her eyes, and this made her so ultimately and absolutely angry that she couldn't speak at all. She got up off Genya's bed and stomped off down the ward between the rows of beds, four on one side, four on the other. She stomped back and stood staring out the window at the mud-colored shapeless ugly world.

Genya was saying something in his gentle, rather reedy voice—"Miriam, honestly, couldn't it be that the metas are worse for me than the native proteins are?"—but she did not understand him; the fear and grief and rage swelled in her and swelled in her and broke, and she cried out, "O Genya, Genya, how could you? Not you, to give up now, after fighting so long—I can't bear it! I can't bear it!" But she did not cry it out aloud. Not one word of it. Never. She screamed in her mind, and some tears came out and ran down her cheeks, but her back was turned to the patient; she looked through distorting tears at the flat valley and the dull sun and said, silent, "I hate you, I hate you, I hate you." Then after a while she could turn around and say coldly, "Lie down"—for he had sat up, distressed by her long silence—"lie down; be quiet. You'll take two metas before dinner. If you need anything, Geza's in the nurse's station." And she walked out.

As she left the infirmary she saw Tina climbing up the back path from the fields, coming to see how Genya was, no doubt. For all his weakness and sickliness Genya had never wanted for girlfriends. Tina, and Shoshanna, and Bella, and Rachel, he could have had his pick. But last year when he and Rachel were living together, he had got condoms from the clinic regularly, and then they had separated; they hadn't married, though by his age, twenty-four, all Settlement kids were married and parents. He hadn't married Rachel, and Miriam knew why. Moral genetics. Bad genes. Non-adaptive. Shouldn't pass them on to the next generation. Weed out the sicklies. No procreation for him, and therefore no marriage; he couldn't ask Rachel to live barren for the love of him. And what the Settlements needed was children, plenty of healthy young natives who, with a little help from the meta pills, could survive on this planet.

Rachel hadn't taken up with anybody else. But she was only eighteen. She'd get over it. Marry a boy from another Settlement, most likely, and move away, away from Genya's big gray eyes. It would be best for her. And for him.

No wonder Genya was suicidal! Miriam thought, and put the thought away from her fiercely, wearily. She was very weary. She had meant to go to her room and wash, change her clothes, change her mood, before dinner; but the room was so lonesome with Leonid away at Salem Settlement and not due back for at least another month, she couldn't stand it. She went straight across the dusty central square of the Settlement to the refectory building, and into the Living Room. To get away, clear away, from the windless haze and the gray sky and the ugly sun.

Nobody was in the Living Room but Commander Marca, fast asleep on one of the padded wooden couches, and Reine, reading. The two oldest members of the Settlement. Commander Marca was in fact the oldest person in the world. He had been forty-four when he piloted the Colony Fleet from Old Earth to New Zion; he was nearly seventy now, and very frail. People did not wear well, here. They aged early, died at fifty, sixty. Reine, the biochemist, was forty-five now, but she looked twenty years older. It's a damned geriatric club,

Miriam thought sourly; and it was true that the young, the Zionborn, seldom used the Living Room. They came there to read, as it held the Settlement's library of books and tapes and microfilm, but not many of them read much, or had much time to read. And maybe the lights, the pictures, made them a little uneasy. They were such moral, severe, serious young people; there was no beauty, no leisure in their lives; how could they approve of this luxury their elders needed, this one haven, this one place like home...

Avram, a wizard with anything electrical, had done the indirect lighting. The big room had no windows at all, but the light was exactly, miraculously, like the light in a room in a house on Earth on a sunny, warm day, maybe in April or early May—clear, bright, gentle. Avram and several others had worked on the pictures, enlarging colored photos to two or three feet square: scenes of Earth, photographs and paintings—Venice, the Negev, the domes of the Kremlin, a farm in Portugal, a village street in England, a beach in Oregon, birch groves in Great Russia, meadows in Poland, cities, forests, mountains, van Gogh's cypresses, Bierstadt's Rocky Mountains, Monet's waterlilies, Leonardo's blue mysterious caves. Every wall of the room was covered with pictures, dozens of pictures, all the beauty of the Earth. So that the Earthborn could see and remember, so that the Zionborn could see and know.

There had been some discussion about the pictures, twenty years ago when Avram had started putting them up: was it really wise? Should we "look back"? And so on. But then Commander Marca had come by on a visit, seen the Living Room of Ararat Settlement, and said, "This is where I'll stay." With every Settlement vying to have him, he had chosen Ararat. Because of the pictures of Earth, because of the light of Earth in that room, shining on the green fields, the snowy peaks, the golden forests of autumn, the flight of gulls above the sea, the white and red and rose of waterlilies on blue pools—clear colors, true, pure, the colors of the Earth.

He slept there now, a handsome old man, the soft light mild on his face. Outside, in the hard, dull, orange sunlight, he would look sick and old, his cheeks veined and muddy. Here you could see what he looked like.

Miriam sat down near him, facing her favorite picture, a quiet spring landscape by Corot, trees over a silvery stream. She was so tired that for once she was willing to just sit, in a kind of stupor. Through the stupor, faintly, idly, words floated. Couldn't it be... Honestly, couldn't it be that the metas are worse... Miriam, honestly, couldn't it be...

"Do you think I never thought of that?" she retorted in silence, getting wrathful again. "Idiot! Do you think I don't know the metas are hard on your guts? Didn't I try fifty different combinations while you were a kid, trying to get rid of the side effects? It's an allergy, that's what it is basically. But it's not as bad as being allergic to the whole damned planet, and that's what we all are! If we don't take the metas, Genya, we starve. Our bodies aren't adapted to the Zion proteins, we get sick, cramps, diarrhoea, convulsions, starvation. You know better than the doctor, do you? Don't give me that. You're trying to—" But she broke off the silent dialogue abruptly. Genya was not trying to kill himself. He was not. He would not. He had courage, that one. And brains.

"All right," she said suddenly in silence. "All right! If you'll stay in the infirmary, under observation—for two weeks, and do exactly what I say—all right, I'll try it!"

Because, said another, even silenter voice deep in her, it doesn't really matter. Whatever you do or don't do, he will die, This year; next year. Two hours; twenty-four years. They are non-adaptives. They can't adjust to this world. And neither can we, neither can we. We weren't meant to live here, Genya my dear. We weren't made for this world, nor it for us. We were made of earth, by earth, to live on earth, under the blue sky and the golden sun.

The dinner gong began to ring. Going into the refectory she met little Shura. The child carried a bunch of the repulsive blackish-purple native weeds, as a child at home would carry a bunch of white daisies, red poppies picked in the fields. Shura's eyes were teary as usual, but she smiled up at "Auntie Doctor." Her lips looked pallid in the red-orange light of sunset through the windows. Everybody's lips looked pallid. Everybody's face looked tired, set, stoical, after the long day's work, as they went into the Settlement dining hall, all together, the three hundred exiles of Ararat on Zion, the eleventh lost tribe.

He was doing very well. She had to admit it. "You're doing well," she said, and he, with his grin, "I told you so!"

"It could be because you're not doing anything else," she said, "smart ass."

"Not doing anything? I filed health records for Geza all morning, I played games with Rosie and Moishe for two hours, I've been grinding colors all afternoon—Say, I need more mineral oil, can I have another litre? It's a much better pigment vehicle than the vegetable oil."

"Sure. But listen, I have something for you better than that. Little Tel Aviv has got their pulp mill going full time. They sent a truck over yesterday with paper—"

"Paper?"

"Half a ton of it! I took two hundred sheets for you. It's in the office." He was off like a shot, and was into the bundle of paper before she even got there. "Oh, God," he said, holding up a sheet, "beautiful, it's beautiful!" And she thought how often she had heard him say that, "beautiful!" of one drab useful thing or another on this world without beauty. The paper was thick, substantial, grayish, in big sheets, intended to be cut small and used sparingly, of course; but let him have it for his painting. There was little enough else she could give him.

"When you let me out of here," Genya said, hugging the bundle of paper like a lover, "I'll go over to Little Tel Aviv and paint their pulp mill, I'll immortalize it!"

"You'd better go lie down."

"No, listen, I promised Moishe I'd beat him at chess. What's wrong with him, anyhow?"

"Allergic reactions. Fainting, edema."

"He's like me?"

Miriam shrugged. "He was fine till this year. Puberty triggered something."

"Take him off metas," Genya said, "and don't let him eat kasha. It always made my eyes swell up."

"Kasha?"

Buckwheat was the one Terran grain that would flourish on New Zion. There were edible native grains, but they had not yet been domesticated long enough to give high yield, and all the Settlements raised buckwheat and ground it into groats and meal.

"I stopped eating it when I was twelve," Genya said, "it never agreed with me."

"Nothing ever agreed with you, idiot."

"Zion mush does. I ate three bowls of it for lunch today."

"He lies around the hospital all day complaining," Miriam said, "and stuffs his belly with that slop. How can an artistic soul eat something that tastes like dirt?"

"You feed it to your helpless child patients in your own hospital! I just ate the leftovers..."

"Oh, get along with you."

"I am. I want to paint while the sun's still up. On a piece of new paper, a whole piece of new paper..."

It had been a long day at the clinic, but there were no in-patients. She had sent Osip home last night in a cast with a good scolding for being so careless as to tip his tractor over, endangering not only his life but the tractor, which was even harder to replace. And young Moishe had gone back to the children's dorm, though she didn't like those traces of edema in his legs. And Rosie was over her asthma, and the Commander's heart was doing as well as could be expected; so the ward was empty, except for her permanent inmate of the past two weeks, Genya.

He was sprawled out on his bed under the window, so lax and deathly still that she had a moment of alarm; but his color was good, he breathed evenly, he was simply asleep—deeply asleep, the way people slept after a hard day in the fields, exhausted.

He had been painting. He had cleaned up the rags and brushes, he always cleaned up promptly and thoroughly, but the picture stood on his makeshift easel. Usually these days he was secretive about his paintings, hid them, since people had stopped admiring them. The Commander murmured to her, "What ugly stuff, poor boy!" But then she had heard young Moishe, watching Genya paint, say, "How do you do it, Genya, how do you make it so pretty?" and Genya answer, "Beauty's in the eye, Moishe."

Well, that was true, and she went closer to look at the painting. It was of the view out the ward window. Not an abstract this time: realistic, all too realistic. Hideously recognizable. There was the flat ridge of Ararat, the mud-colored trees and fields, the gray sky, the storage barn and a corner of the school building in the foreground. Her eyes went from the painted scene to the real one. To spend hours, days, painting that! What a waste, what a waste.

It was hard on Genya, it was sad, the way he hid his paintings now, knowing that nobody would want to see them, except maybe a child like Moishe fascinated with the mere skill of the hand, the craftsman's dexterity.

That night as Genya helped her straighten up the injection cabinets—he was a great deal of help around the infirmary these days—she said, "I like the picture you painted today."

"I finished it today," he corrected her. "Damn thing took all week."

"Can I put it up in the Living Room?"

He looked at her across a tray of hypodermic needles, his eyes quiet and a little quizzical. "In the Living Room? But that's all pictures of Home."

"It's time maybe we had some pictures of our new home there."

"A moral gesture, eh? Sure, OK. If you like it."

"I like it very much," she lied blandly.

"It isn't bad," he said. "I'll do better, though, now that I know what I'm doing."

"You take it over tomorrow and put it up. Artists are always so touchy about where they get their pictures hung, and the lighting. Besides, it's time you were getting out. A little. An hour or two a day. No more."

"Can I eat dinner in the dining hall, then?"

"All right. It'll keep Tina from always coming here to keep you from being lonely and eating up all the infirmary rations. That girl eats like a vacuum pump. Listen, if you go out in the middle of the day, will you kindly wear a hat?"

"You think I'm right, then."

"Right?"

"That I do better without metas."

"I have no idea. You've been all right before, for weeks, and then poof, down again. Nothing whatever has been proved."

"Except that I've lived a month without metas, and gained six pounds."

"And edema of the head, Mr. Know-It-All?"

She saw him the next day sitting with Rachel, just before dinner-time, on the slope below the storage barn. Rachel had not come to see him in the infirmary. They sat side by side, very close together, motionless, not talking.

Miriam went on to the Living Room. A half hour there before dinner had become a habit with her lately, it seemed to rest her from the weariness of the day. But it was less peaceful than usual this evening. The Commander was awake, and talking with Reine and Avram. "Well, where did it come from then?" he was saying in his heavy Italian accent—he had not learned Hebrew till he was forty. "Who put it there?" Then seeing Miriam he greeted her as always with splendid cordiality of voice and gesture—"Ah, Doctor! Please, join us, come, solve our mystery for us. You know each picture in this room as well as I. Where, do you think, and when did we acquire the new one? You see?"

"It's Genya's," Miriam was about to say, when she saw the new picture. It wasn't Genya's. It was a painting, all right, but a landscape of the Earth: a wide valley, the fields green and green-gold, orchards coming into flower, the sweeping slope of a mountain in the distance, a tower, perhaps a castle or medieval farm-building, in the foreground, and over all the pure and subtle blue of the sunlit sky. It was a complex, vigorous, and happy painting, a celebration of the spring, an act of praise.

"How beautiful," she said, her voice catching. "Didn't you put it up, Avram?"

"Me? I can photograph, I can't paint. Look at it, it's genuine, some kind of tempera or oils on paper, see?"

"Somebody brought it from Home. Had it in their baggage," Reine suggested.

"For twenty-five years?" said the Commander. "Why? And who? We all know what all the others have!"

"No. I think," Miriam was confused, and stammered, "I think it's something Genya did. I asked him to put up one of his paintings. Not this one. How did he do this?"

"Copied from a photograph," Avram suggested.

"No no no no, impossible!" old Marca said, outraged. "No, that is a painting, not a copy! That is a work of art, that was seen, seen with the eyes and the heart!"

With the eyes and the heart.

Miriam looked, and she saw. She saw what the light of NSC 641 had hidden from her, what the artificial Earthlight of the room revealed to her. She saw what Genya saw.

"I think it must be in Central France, the Auvergne," Reine was saying wistfully, and the Commander, "O no no no, it's near Lake Como, certainly," and Avram, "I thought it might have been painted in the Caucasus," when they all turned to look at Miriam. She had made a strange little noise, a gasp or laugh or sob. "It's here," she said. "Here. That's Ararat. The mountain. That's the fields, our fields, our trees. That's the corner of the school, that tower. It's here. This place. It's how Genya sees it. With the eyes and the heart."

"But the trees are green, the sky's blue, Miriam. It's Earth—"

"Yes! It's Earth. Genya's Earth!"

"But he can't—"

"How do you know? How do we know what a child of Zion sees? We can see it in this artificial light. Take it outside, into the daylight, and you'll see what we always see, the ugly colors, the ugly planet where we're not at home. But he is at home! He is! It's we," Miriam said, laughing in tears, looking at them all, the anxious, tired, elderly faces, "*we* who are the non-adaptives. We with our meta pills—we can survive here, barely. But don't you see, he *lives* here? He and the others, the sicklies. Maybe on Earth they would have been non-adaptives, allergics, but here—And for twenty-five years I've been feeding them metas, idiot! Idiot! Oh! He and Rachel can marry— They've got to marry, he should have kids—And Moishe, thank God! there's a new one—Listen, I must go talk to Genya and Rachel, immediately. Excuse me!" She left, a short gray woman moving like a lightning bolt.

Marca, Avram, and Reine stood staring after her, at each other, and finally back at the painting.

It hung there before them, serene and joyful, full of light.

"I don't understand," said Avram.

"Non-adaptive?" Reine said thoughtfully.

"It is very beautiful," said the old Commander of the Colony Fleet. "Only, it makes me homesick."

The Workshopping

Thirteen of the original Booth Lodge group were convened at the editor's apartment on a pleasant Sunday afternoon, the object being to workshop Ursula's story.

On their arrival, each was given a copy of the story which they then proceeded to read. When everyone had arrived, read the story, and had at least half an hour to mull it over, the workshopping began.

The entire proceedings lasted close to two hours and were put onto tape. A copy of this was posted to Ursula in England, and her written reply is in response to this tape.

The remaining six of the original group who were unable to attend the workshopping—mainly for geographical reasons—were sent copies of Ursula's story and asked to contribute concise written critiques. These have been placed at the end of the workshopping.

What follows is a concise rendering of that extraordinary two hours, with redundancies and repetitions removed and, I hope, all the vital criticisms preserved.

(*Publisher's Note:* Throughout this section, page numbers refer to pages in the original manuscript, not to pages in this edition.)

EDWARD MUNDIE: It's hard to pick up—being at the start—but the thing that impressed me most about the first part of the story was how much it reached out from a central point and grasped at the background and all the matters relating to the story. Now this happens in a lot of stories, but it was particularly noticeable in this one how all the pertinent facts of the story related to your central point, and how much use was made of metaphors and illustrations— you seemed to have no lack of either: they were popping out all over the place, to bring out all the points you wanted to make. I felt that the greatest strength in the early part of the story was these settings and descriptions, that stood out very clearly. I found the story very interesting; it held my attention. To me it was done in pastels rather than in bright colors: the dramatic scenes at the end seemed very subdued; the whole setting and description was done with a great deal of restraint. One comment I could make upon the story in that vein is that I thought the ending could possibly have taken a more dramatic tone, and got away from the paler colors of the rest of the story and given us a more powerful ending, to underline the twist, the reversal, the other aspect of the "eye opening." I think that's all I'd like to say at this stage.

PIP MADDERN: First off, I loved the story. I like the idea of the artist being, as it were, the community's "eye." I think the title is beautiful: "The Eye Altering" just catches it perfectly. Something that did worry me—I think it is possibly dealt with in the story, but it still struck me as a trifle inconsistent, that Genya should ever have been treated as so unhealthy. I presume the idea was that, since his mother was having trouble adapting to New Zion, and he himself was premature, he was unhealthy from that point of view. But it did make me wonder if children adapting to a new planet would not in fact be healthier when born than children who weren't adapting to the new planet, and therefore wouldn't get so immediately struck on drugs of all kinds. Then perhaps the situation as depicted would never have arisen. Of course this analysis may be wide open for criticism, but it was something that struck me. One other thing: I missed out a bit on the real view of the colonists. Miriam has it, but Miriam is in a sense the weak link between Genya and the older people who are not adapting: I wished I could have heard a little more from the commander, and the biologist, because we didn't really hear much from them except right at the end, and although their character was implied continually through their nostalgia and blindness to the beauties, it wasn't perhaps something that you always saw. But perhaps I'm asking for a novel rather than a short story? Just a nit: on p.9 where you talk about Miriam thinking, "'Do you think I never thought of that?' she said, getting wrathful again." That "getting wrathful again" didn't seem to me to be necessary. You could see herself working herself up, answering her inner doubts; it seemed to be an intrusion by the author that wasn't really necessary. But apart from that I don't think I've got very much to say: I loved it.

STEFAN VUCAK: I agree with some of the points raised by Ted and Pip, but I felt there was a very slow start to the story. Being a short story I feel that you should grip the reader's attention, his imagination, before you begin to develop the plot. And here you have, say, four to five pages which are devoted to describing their environment, and to some extent the characters, and I felt that far more work was needed to make these characters stand out, so that the reader could either sympathize with them or hate them—or something. But they seem to stand aloof from their surroundings: I just couldn't feel close to them. Nor does there seem to be a very strong framework to the story: there's a lot of space devoted to talking about the pills and whether or not they are beneficial, but there's nothing you can actually *grasp* on to see how the story is developing. And, as Pip mentioned, the children being born on this planet should be more adaptive. I also feel that with a major expedition to another planet such as this, where conditions are so different from Earth, these factors would have been considered. That the colonists would have to depend on pills rather than, say, "terraforming" the planet is a little hard to take. A few minor points: on p.5 you say "Genya, my dear, what do you mean? It's no good?" Then the next line says, "'It's no good,' he said." This is just repetition; it irritated me; it was unnecessary. And on p.10: "He is doing very well," and on the next line "She had to admit, he was doing well." Slightly out of place, I thought. But for the moment, I think I'll leave it at that.

DAVID GRIGG (interjecting): Can I just make a comment on this thing that both Pip and Stefan said? I didn't see this adaptivity of the colonists as a problem. Ursula has made quite clear that they could not get protein from the food on the planet unless they took the pills; if this was so for the original colonists then naturally they would also give their children the pills, otherwise they would starve to death. So I don't really see this as a technical criticism.

BRUCE GILLESPIE: My first reaction—and I read the story quite quickly—was perhaps that it was your tribute to Australia. It's the best summary of the European attitude toward Australia apart from some of Patrick White's work that I've seen, and on p.13, there's Genya's painting: "It was a view out of the ward window. Not an abstract. Realistic, all too realistic. Hideously recognizable. The flat ridge of Ararat, the mud-colored trees and fields, the gray skies, the storage barn, etc." This is so much the reaction of Europeans to Australia that I am wondering if you somehow picked this up while you were here—I don't even know if it was written since your visit. As for the story itself, I felt it was a bit long, a bit overwritten, there was a bit too much repetition. Especially when compared to some of your recent stories. But apart from that I think it's very effective—particularly toward the end. The last page comes off very well. I thought the use of metaphors which tied in almost exclusively with painting—which was fairly clear from about the second page onward—was an excellent way of binding together all the images. That's all for the moment.

DAVID GRIGG: I liked the story very much: I found it very evocative and it carried a great deal of feeling, and that was very valuable. I thought there were quite a few technical faults but before I go onto them there are one or two other things I'd like to mention. The whole thing about the colonists being Jewish and coming to a planet and calling it New Zion was slightly off-putting. The last line of the first paragraph, "Oh Jerusalem, if I forget thee," was really a sort of emotional cliché. A few pages later she's saying, "Remember oranges, the oranges of Haifa, the sweet juice on the tongue." I don't know, but it just felt a little bit overdone to me, because in the rest of the story the Jewishness just doesn't come out anywhere near as much. Apart from that, I guessed the ending coming: about p.7 or so when the boy starts to talk about feeling better off the pills—that sort of telegraphed the ending for me. But perhaps that was only accidental. The other criticisms are more technical. For example, I find it a little contrived that none of Genya's paintings have ever been seen before in artificial light of any sort. Also, he was originally doing conventional portraits that people must have liked. I find it strange that he should suddenly change; I would have assumed that his vision would have been different from birth. I also find it a little contrived that there is only this one living room where the light matches the light of Earth. It is crucial to the story that his painting has to be hung there before the "difference" can be seen. Otherwise I think it's a very nice story.

ANDREW WHITMORE: I don't know: I think either the story is too short or too long. If it's just a sort of gimmick story, then it is too long, because you can guess what's going to happen. But if it's going to be a story about either the artist or the people on New Zion, then it's far too short, because we don't really learn anything about, for example, what the artist thinks or feels about his painting. I think this is very important in relation to your other stories, where it is the people who come through to the reader: what they think and what they feel, and you don't really get that in this story . . . not very much, anyway. I haven't really anything more to add, except for a few technical criticisms. The sort of dialogue on p.9—that section where she's "getting wrathful." I thought that was contrived: there are other ways it could have been done, like holding a conversation in her head . . . or something. But I guess "contrived" sums up my whole feeling about the story. And it seems too long.

DERRICK ASHBY: I agree that the story seems contrived, but just the same it seems to work. The others have mentioned that the ending is telegraphed, and that's true enough, but that's mainly because everything in the story is working from this central point: of course you can see what's going to happen. But in getting to the point there are these little inconsistencies, such as the kids being put on the pills—things like that. Stefan criticized the slow introduction—the description of the planet and the colonists in their relation to it—but I think this is essential, because you see the planet through the colonists' eyes, and it tells you a lot about their actual character. And you get a contrast between what the original colonists see and what the later generation sees. I also like the irony of the story: it's the non-adaptives who don't need to adapt and yet the colonists are trying to make them adapt.

BARBARA COLEMAN: I enjoyed the story, and one of the things I enjoyed was the pictorial descriptions. I don't think the beginning is at all slow: I liked all the description of the planet—particularly that on p.2. It sets the scene perfectly: you can understand what Miriam is grumbling about. Once again, I don't agree with Pip and Stefan on their criticism of the "weak" children. It seems reasonable enough to me that children born on another planet, while appearing weak by our standards, would have adapted to their environment in a way their parents could not. One point: we have no actual description of Miriam, and although most of the action takes place around her and in her mind, I'd like to know more about Miriam herself, as a person. The only thing we do know about her is that she has had repeated miscarriages; we don't know anything about her husband or her friends. I would certainly like to have known a little more about the other main characters, too. Now, a couple of nits to pick: I'm sure the Israelis use metric measurements, and these people sound as though they're Israelis. One bit I do like very much is on p.5, where Genya decides he's not going to take the pills any more and Miriam gets most insulted about it: I can picture that happening; it rings true. But to reiterate: I think this is a very pictorial story: you can feel it unrolling in your mind. And that's its main strength.

ANNIS SHEPHERD: First of all, the things I liked about your story. I adore the title: it's very euphonious, "The Eye Altering." I love the idea where beauty is in the eye of the beholder, not only as far as the artist is concerned but also as far as the colonists are concerned. Also the fact that we appreciate what we know and understand: that also comes over very strongly. Whereas that which is alien can be seen as being ugly—wasn't that how you said some visitors see Australia, Bruce? I think that we see people in the next street that way, to be quite frank. My main criticism—and this differs from what some of the others have said—is that the story is too short, and for this reason: we have so much information about this world, New Zion—and very interesting information—that I think it has to be balanced by a greater depth of characterization, if it is to work. Too much background is annoying in this case, so you either cut back on the world-information, and make it shorter—as someone has suggested—or you expand your characters and create a longer work. I personally would prefer the latter: I would like to get to know more about the feelings of the characters, in particular Miriam and Genya. My major criticism could be said to be a result of this lack: on p.16 her recognition or understanding of Genya is just too quick. I don't think she could have grasped all that he saw, so quickly. To me the ending was too telescoped. And I agree with the others in that the ending is just too subdued: I like a dramatic ending, but that's just a personal preference, after all. Several people have commented on the fact that the ending was telegraphed. Well this all depends on what you think the central point was: if it was whether or not the people could survive without the pills, then you could say that the ending was predictable. But to me the central point is the recognition that there is beauty in the world, and that however alien it is to that person, it remains beautiful—to me that is the central point of the story, and when it does come as a twist at the ending, it does so as a surprise . . . for me, anyway.

ROB GERRAND: I'm going to be very critical of this story, Ursula. It held my attention and I enjoyed reading it, but I think that's more a tribute to your power as a writer than to the structure. I'm tempted to suspect that you might have written it deliberately as a story to be workshopped; in other words you made more of a first draft attempt at it than you would have normally. First of all, I think there was a major flaw in your choice of a narrator: Miriam is the person whose viewpoint we share throughout the story; and yet Miriam is the sort of person who can say "Oh Jerusalem, if I forget thee"—a very literary sort of allusion—who can be remembering the sweet juice of an orange on her tongue, and who is also the rest of the time, a practical sort, not the kind of person who seems to have a universal understanding of people, not the type given to literary allusion. She seems inconsistent. But we must see the planet and its people through her eyes. A structural flaw is that the whole thing seems to be based on a genetic change in the children, but you give no basis for why a child should be genetically different from its parents. And why should Genya have worried about having a child with Rachel? Just because he was born premature and half dead from cyanosis—that's not a genetic fault in either case, and there is no reason why he could not have bred as true as any other person in the colony. Or why couldn't they have lived together and Rachel been impregnated by someone else? Another thing: these people have been on this planet for 25 years. You say, on p.8, "people did not wear well here; they aged early, died at 50 or 60." I don't think you could generalize to know, after only 25 years, the average age at which people would die. And you have the Commander alive at 72. To me the strength of the story seems to depend on these genetic factors, and the fact that the painting is seen for the first time in artificial light is a sort of symbolic way of summarizing what the story is about, but because you've written the story to depend on these gimmicks or facts you have weakened it. I think you could have done without them. I also think you could have done without the Jewishness. Now, you have them on New Zion, but nowhere in the story are any of the people particularly Jewish. It seems to me there is no basis for calling them Jewish or having them Jewish unless you give some reason for it; this rang false to me. Nor are the characters sufficiently realized, as Annis pointed out; we don't know much about Genya or Miriam as people. Now a few nits: you describe the sun as "warty as an orange." To me a wart and an orange are very different things; I don't know what you're trying to say; it just doesn't conjure up anything in my mind. In the same passage you talk about the sun staring down and you staring up, "with an idiot's unrecognizing stare": if this idiot's stare is yours or the sun's—that's another criticism—it seems an over-written phrase: an idiot is capable of recognition. There's another cliché on p.5, "heard her voice as rough as a wood rasp"; that seems almost as though it was put in for us to pick out. And on p.6 "so ultimately and absolutely angry that she couldn't speak at all. She got off Genya's bed and stomped down the hall." Then she stomps back. I think all this could have been handled with more subtlety and with greater force. I am also wondering why these people would be relying on condoms as a contraceptive device: I would like to think they had access to something more aesthetic and effective. Another thing that surprised me was when she said, on p.10, "Oh, he wouldn't be trying to kill himself. He had courage that one, and brains." I don't see how having brains or having courage has anything to do with the prospensity to commit suicide. Sylvia Plath had both brains and courage, but she suicided. If anything, such qualities might lead one into a situation of self-doubt. Animals tend not to commit suicide. On p.10 again, "Because, said another even silenter voice deep in her." Silence is absolute. I think you meant "quieter." And on p. 17: "She leapt, a short, gray woman moving like a lightning bolt." That may not be a subjunctive tension, but it is a cliché. Others have brought up the matter of Genya's paintings never having been seen in artifical light before—that sort of gimmicking with the story interferes with what you're trying to say, I think. I've been pretty harsh on it, Ursula, mainly because I don't think it compares well with most of the other stories of yours I have read.

GRAEME LUNN: I haven't quite had long enough to digest this story, so naturally enough my feelings for it have been colored by the criticisms of those before me. I did enjoy it. I enjoyed the leisurely unfolding of the plot, and I can't agree that the ending was telegraphed, because I took the story to be a portrait with very interesting mechanical versus natural imagery. I didn't find any difficulty with the viewpoint-through-Miriam, whom I saw as a rather sensitive mind, more or less lacquered over by NSC 641. I agree with what Ted said in the very beginning that although the use of watercolors could be very appropriate to the depressed conditions, perhaps the reactions of the characters could have been stronger. I thought there were a few clichés, which Rob has already dealt with. I did have a slightly negative reaction to the "Jerusalem" imagery, and I didn't think the idea of the pills was very practical: just another image of the adult world repressing the young, and we've had enough of that on Earth. Perhaps this was something you meant to imply?

RANDAL FLYNN: I liked the story very much. You do seem to have begun with several central features and built the story to include them. It makes the story very functional in its plot elements. My ears pricked up at what Annis said about there being "beauty in the world," and that it is the function of the artist to record it. Your story immediately brought to mind Joyce Cary's *The Horse's Mouth,* and I settled down and followed it through at that level and enjoyed it. I thought Miriam's inability to understand Genya on p.5 was unconvincing, because *we* could, and she should also. There have been various comments about the ending. For me it stood out from the rest of the story; I found it very dramatic. This also gives an indication of the inconsistency in Miriam's character: here she sees the picture and everything becomes clear in her mind, as it does in ours. This feeling should have been equally true elsewhere in the story. About the society: I received a vague first impression of it, and this was carried through and grew until I now have a silent picture of the world. It's a very quiet world, isn't it? I don't recall any birds, or rivers, or even the sound a breeze makes, but then this is part of the picture of New Zion, and I enjoyed it: it reminded me very much of Annares. I liked the beginning very much: very peaceful, wistful, tranquil. Then it moved up in pace toward the end: I was really excited by the time I reached the last page. I especially liked the scene where the young Shura is carrying the blackish-purple flowers, and the comparison with Earth. These points, spaced here and there throughout the story, are very effective. Most of the nits have already been picked: but on p.4 the description of the use of the metas is a minor expository lump that could better be worked into the prose less obtrusively. You know they are going to play some important role in the climax—and they do—and I think you could have immersed this fact a little more into the story.

KITTY VIGO: Well, I didn't find many nits to pick, but perhaps that's got a lot to do with the way I reacted to the story. The recurring image I had all the way through the story was—is it a Taoist one?—of the Buddhist monk dreaming he was a butterfly dreaming he was a man. To me it was a story about perception, and how one thing can be many things depending on the point of view you take. I was reminded, in this context, of Chris Priest's *Inverted World,* which seems to work in that fashion, and this in turn led me to wonder if perhaps "The Eye Altering" is a story about fast changes, and if you're writing a story about fast changes, is it altogether that necessary to have lots of well delineated characters? Yet somehow it seemed wrong that the action was compressed into two weeks: it should have taken much longer, because realizations often don't come quickly. I think that's the only real fault I found with the story. I liked it very much, and that juxtaposition of images that Genya should be sick and yet be healthy, while Miriam should be healthy and yet be sick—I found that fascinating. Oh, and that business about the Jewishness. Perhaps we have a very clichéd view of what Jewishness is, and I don't think it really mattered all that much that the people should be more Jewish than they were. Should they have all talked with a Jewish-Bronx accent? Would that have made them more convincing?

The Workshopping: The Written Responses from Interstate:

JOHN EDWARD CLARK: The problem with criticizing any of Ursula's stories is that all you can really do is nit-pick. So here's mine: 1. The colony has been established for over 25 years. Surely in all that time someone would have realized that the colors were similar to Earth colors under a different light? One would only have to go outside at night with a flashlight to see for example, that the grass and trees were green. 2. When Miriam agrees to allow Genya's painting to be hung in the living room, I think she accepts too readily. That room was almost sacred to her and the others. I think at first she would at least have tried to dissuade Genya from hanging the painting there. 3. Surely the lights in the buildings at night would have revealed the colors of the painting were similar to those of Earth? 4. I would have liked to know what the purpose of the colony was. It has been established over 25 years: 300 people, living close to subsistence level and all seeming to hate the planet. I wonder what they were doing there? 5. The scientists must have been pretty dumb to take so long to realize the metas were adversely affecting the newborn. 6. Miriam seems to have hated this world for the past 25 years. If the others thought that way, I don't see how the colony could have endured so long. Human beings are adaptive; I think they would have stopped hating the place after a few years. 7. "I hate you, I hate you, I hate you"—p.6—seems out of character. More like something a child would say. 8. On p.12 Miriam seems somewhat surprised to learn that kasha has always made Genya's eyes swell up. Yet I would have thought, having been his doctor for 24 years, she would have been familiar with this condition.

PETRINA SMITH: The most obvious criticisms are those of "early draft" awkwardness. There are explanations (paras. 4, 7 and 8) and descriptions (para. 2) that might be condensed, and an overall looseness. However, despite this the story is structurally sound. I liked the "visual" motif, especially the watercolor description (para. 3): that really worked—a vivid impression of a desolate landscape rather than a description of it. The constant hints about the importance of lighting were artfully planted: Commander Marca's different appearance in different lighting and Moishe's exchange with Genya about his painting. So the ending wasn't a rabbit-out-of-a-hat, and neither was it given away in advance. Some random points: the impression is given that Genya was always like this, so why wasn't it noticed before? Hadn't Genya ever been in the living room? He said how beautiful some things around New Zion were—hadn't this ever provoked any curiosity? And perhaps it could have been explained that "kasha" and "buckwheat" are one and the same: it took a while for me to realize this, and also that "Zion mush" was native to the planet. Miriam is described only at the end—by this time I had a different mental picture of her. The ending did seem a little uncontrolled and over-emotional, and I felt this lessened the impact. For all this, the story gripped me and on a first reading I forgot altogether that I should be criticizing it. I suppose that's an indication of a good story. I really liked it.

BRUCE BARNES: On New Zion, how could Genya possibly paint *blue* sky and *green* trees, when such light wavelengths would be filtered out by the cloud layer? No matter how well adapted to the planet he is, Genya could never see colors that were not there—and the plot relies on his ability to do this! Even so, "Auntie Doc" displays a remarkable lack of a proper scientific attitude—"seeing the truth" with not much data to go on, thereby risking potentially nasty mistakes resulting from erroneous conclusions acted upon too hastily. And why are the children so well adapted to the new planet? Even with the high infant mortality rate suggested, how is it that the survivors are just the right sort of "on Earth...non-adaptives, allergics," to thrive so well on this alien world? If the original colonists were so poorly adaptive, why then did they ever choose to become colonists? And is the Jewish angle significant? As far as I can see, this only made the story unnecessarily complicated. Having to work out that "kasha" was buckwheat was worse than being skidded to a halt by a subjunctive tension. Of course you could argue that the colors of the painting matched Earth-normal only by woolly coincidence, and that the colonists were involuntary (or voluntary) exiles, and so on, but surely a writer's job is to settle all this in the story, not leave matters so important hanging in the air for the reader to find excuses for. If the reader does this, he may feel like writing *all* the story.

ROBERT YOUNG: Overall I was impressed by the story. The idea of the painting appearing to be different under different lighting conditions was a masterly stroke. Miriam came across to me as a very real and believable person; her feelings were very well described. One thing that bothered me was the section beginning "settling slowly" down to "splendor." Since there would be no clouds to pick up the colors from the sun and so end the day in splendor, perhaps this should read "settling slowly onto the horizon"? The major fault seems to lie in the scene where Miriam asks Genya if she can put up his painting in the living room. No reason is given for this action. Miriam hates the picture, it is very likely that the others will also dislike it, so this seems totally out of character. Having the painting viewed under "Earthlight" is the key point in the plot, and the events leading up to it should be convincingly explained. Perhaps it would be better if the painting found its way into the room in a more subtle way—possibly by Genya taking it there to show the Commander. But apart from this major criticism, I thought the story well structured and very rewarding to read.

After the individual comments people took up various points with each other. It would be impossible to capture the excitement and vigor of this debate—and space does not permit—but it is important to note that the following points were made, of which the two major ones dealt with the "genetic" background and the "Jewishness" of the colonists:

EDWARD MUNDIE felt that the criticisms of repetition were unfounded. While against repetition himself, he felt that in this case Ursula had used it as a technique to underline and in some cases heighten a point. ROB GERRAND brought up the use of insulin with diabetics for genetic reasons, and compared this with the colonists taking their metas, but maintained that the strength of the story did not rest on this genetic factor, so why have it? The story is really about the individual's concept of the world and "the eye altering." BARBARA COLEMAN made the point that the Jewish people are "professional exiles," and this was expanded upon by PIP MADDERN, who felt that that was why the colonists had to be a Jewish community and a Jewish story. DAVID GRIGG disagreed: he thought that was making things "too easy." He felt that the same feeling of longing—the "Oh, Jerusalem thing" as it had come to be called—could have been achieved by some other means. PIP kept putting forward her conviction that it *had* to be Jewish: the whole feeling of the kibbutz was there. The argument grew: DAVID said that the "oranges of Haifa" incident was about the only Jewish thing in the story. ANNIS interjected: "I remember somebody stressing at Booth Lodge that if you are going to inject something into the early part of your story—say a glove lying on the road—then it should have some connection to the story. It must be pertinent. So if we have references to a Jewish community on the opening page, I feel that this should have some pertinence to the remainder of the story." DAVID felt that the whole kibbutz thing fell down in the section where the room and paintings were described: only *one* of the paintings has anything to do with Jerusalem. The debate moved to exiles in general, for example the Boers and the American pioneers, and how they thought constantly of their homelands as they carved up the wilderness. ANNIS reminded everyone that the Mormons, in the U.S., used to call the mountains Old Zion, and were always referring back to Jerusalem. ROB took up this tack and stuck doggedly to his guns on the matter of characterization: that merely being a Melburnian was to be a special sort of person, and that anyone who has met people from other races, or even people from places in other countries, will have realized that they all have a distinct character. And they must be characterized, not merely given labels. TED MUNDIE drew everyone's attention to the fact that Ursula may have simply chosen her colonists to be Jewish because they would have already proved that they could get on together as a closed community. KITTY objected to the fact that everyone seemed to want cliché-Jews. A general agreement was reached that it was the matter of *consistency* that was the object of the debate: was Ursula's use of her Jewish colonists consistent? ANNIS offered an excellent analogue: after announcing something she did not expect any of them to know—that she was a Mormon—she then went on to expound how her religion colored her everyday life. In certain situations, this becomes very evident. "If I go to a party, I don't drink or smoke." After enumerating similar instances, she referred the group again to ROB's main objection, that the Jewishness *did not come out in the story,* through the thoughts or actions of the characters, and that this was probably why the story was under-characterized. It wasn't enough to mention the name of a mountain range, she insisted: the feeling has to come out of the characters. At this juncture DAVID was growing restless and asked to move the topic along: he said that while a number of people had complained about the ending he, like Randal, loved the underplaying. ANNIS qualified her initial dissatisfaction with the ending, mainly over her usage of the word "dramatic." She felt the central or next to central character should be involved in the ending. Genya, the artist, was not present, and the last line was not spoken by Miriam, but by a subsidiary and rather unimportant character the reader had not identified with. ROB objected to Miriam referring to Genya as a "sickly," feeling it was used in a derogatory manner. PIP disagreed, and felt that this gave the reader an insight into Miriam's maternal nature. STEFAN discovered another small nit: G-class stars are not orange, he says. This led the discussion into a long and very thoughtful debate upon what the group considered another bothersome failing of the story: the "gimmicky" lighting situation that made Genya's painting "visible" in only one room. ANNIS brought the discussion to a close, remarking how marvelous it would have been for the reader to have felt Genya's reactions to seeing his painting in Earthlight, and how much more dramatic to have witnessed the ending from his viewpoint. On this moot point, the discussion of "The Eye Altering" was concluded.

URSULA K. LE GUIN: I am just batting this off from the notes I took while listening to the tape. Incoherent notes, decorated with doodles of gum-trees. What a strange and wonderful two hours! Ted Mundie, you nearly made me cry *again,* when your voice came on and there was all Booth Lodge around me all at once ... but I shut my eyes and saw your faces and soon it seemed perfectly natural, just another session of the workshop, threads of careful argument entangled suddenly in wild snarls, snorts of disgust and laughter, polar contradictions of opinion combining unexpectedly into a whole new conception ... Oof, I'm exhausted, it *must* be lunchtime!

Two preliminaries: No, Bruce, it was written before I ever saw Australia; and Australia isn't like New Zion even to this unaltered eye, it is strange not drab, sad not dreary, beautiful not ugly. And no, Rob, I didn't deliberately write a lousy story for a workshop to work on; the implication is flattering, but alas ...

The essential flaw, as I see it, is this: I totally failed to get across to you (that is, to have perfectly clear in my own mind while writing) that what is involved is not a genetic *change,* but a genetic *capacity:* that in fact the underlying concept is not genetics at all, but allergy.

Some people (including myself to a mild degree) are allergic to sunlight. Only a cloudy climate or a hard-earned tan saves them from becoming a mass of lumps and itches all summer. Now that is bizarre, to be allergic to the sun, the source of life on earth. When ashamed of my rashes, I have wondered if perhaps some other sun, a milder one, would fail to bring out this allergy-reaction. Same idea as putting babies who react allergically to cow's milk onto goat's milk—or preventing the reaction from ever getting established by starting the baby on human milk.

Now the leap I made was to consider normal reaction (to milk, sunlight, or whatever) as adaptedness, and allergic reaction as maladaptedness; and then (second leap) to ask, what if all allergies were in fact capacities—misadaptations to Earth circumstances, but potential adaptedness to slightly different circumstances? A key that fits a slightly different lock, as it were? A silly notion, but I think it has a proper heady scent of the true Pseudo-Scientific Garbage.

The trouble lies in the use of the word "adaptation," which can imply *change*—alteration to fit existing circumstances. I was talking about a ready-made adaptation. Obviously the word's got to go, or at least be used unambiguously.

Somebody brought up a parallel to insulin in the "meta" pills, and that's right on the nail. If we all became diabetics (through either a genetic or an environmental change), we'd all take insulin, habitually and without question: exactly as we now all "take" protein or, if we can't, die. (NB: There are some people who can't eat protein. Until modern medicine, they were either sicklies, or they died.) However, it was also correct to bring up the point that really the doctors of New Zion would be far more suspicious of the metas, more ready to test and vary. I can't figure out how to get this flaw out of the story. A discovery should not have to rest upon a stupidity. It often does, in stories; seldom in reality.

Anyhow, so long as it's not clear that no Lamarckian change has taken place, but that a genetic capacity (which on Earth, and under the "terraforming" effect of metas, is a defect) has been potentiated—so long as that's not clear, the connection between Genya's "sickliness" and his paintings remains obscure. It won't be easy to make clear, either, because, although Genya is "adapted" to New Zion by nature, still, when he stops taking the metas to which he is allergic and which thus "misadapt" him, he really wouldn't recover all at once. He would have to learn to see what he had only glimpsed before, and to learn to paint it. Miriam and the other Earthborns see the beauty of the painting at once, because they have seen beauty before (the beauty of Earth, of course, which is all they can see; they are "allergic" to the beauty of New Zion). But Genya really has hardly had a chance to see the beauty of his world; he learns to see and paint it improbably fast. Oh dear, oh dear.

About Jewishness. A fascinating discussion. Annis and Pip, I think it was, are right: the characters are Jewish because Jews are "professional exiles"—all the right feeling-tone was there ready-made, I could use reference instead of exposition. But I did not make it clear that these people did not choose exile, but were exiled. By whom? Well, you can read in an Arab-dominated Earth; or a Soviet-dominated Earth; or what you please—no lack of anti-Semitic groups to choose from, I fear. This is why the colonists are on a semi-habitable planet. They didn't choose it: they escaped or were driven off to it. Also, this is why they're from all over, not only from Israel (and that's why the paintings of Earth are from all over, not just Israel. There are, after all, Jews in England, Russia, Oregon, New York, etc). As for the objection Rob had, that the characters don't "act Jewish . . ." Sigh. Do my black characters, like Genly Ai in *Left Hand of Darkness,* act black, I wonder? Do my human characters act human? God knows. I will point out that two people at PSU, and David here, observed gently that Miriam's emotionality is perhaps too "ethnic" in places. Perhaps, since none of us is Jewish, we should leave this to Jewish readers; and if they want merely to say that I've got a hell of a lot of chutshpeh, they may well be right, but I wish they'd tell me how to spell chutshpeh. [*Chutzpah—ed.*]

About the lighting. Stefan's right, this is gimmicky. Also, I didn't seem to get it through, despite a rather elaborate description, that only in *that one room* is the lighting a deliberate, "exact" reproduction of Earth sunlight. Of course they've got normal electric lights elsewhere in the settlement; those can be ignored. The point is, Miriam sees the picture first in New Zion daylight; then in Earth daylight. Only in the latter can she "see" it at all. (To Genya, by the way, it would look rather ugly, in the Living Room.)

Nits and Comments: I intend to act upon many of the nits, especially Pip's, Barbara's, Randal's, Rob's. Annis, you're right about the main-characters-offstage ending, but I'm not sure I can change it, it still feels right to me. Stefan, my consultant astronomer assured me there are orange G-class stars. Rob, "sickly" is derogatory or patronizing when used by a healthy colonist, but of course Pip's right, Miriam uses it maternally and doctorishly, in all affection. Rob again: Sylvia Plath is not the kind of person a middle-aged doctor in frontier surroundings would be likely to admire; where survival is genuinely at stake, suicides do not become heroes. Ted and Graeme, what you say about pastels and watercolors is true; to be consistent, Genya should paint only in watercolor, but oh well. By the way, Damon Knight turned the story down, and his main objection to it was that you cannot, he said, paint in oils on paper! He said he'd tried. So have I. Worked fine for me. Depends on the paper, obviously. Sigh.

THE CHARACTER STORIES

Randal Flynn

Stabbed Alive

> *'Now he's been stabbed alive.*
> *He's seeing things.'*
> Joyce Cary: *The Horse's Mouth*

On August 2nd, 1975, the mundane world disappeared and stayed away for a week. In its place, drastically contracted and reduced from the real world, was the world of Booth Lodge.

There were nineteen aspiring and unpublished writers gathered together for the workshop. I don't know who made the beds or watered the flowers, or who maintained the place; certainly our meals appeared regularly before us from out of a shifting gray shimmer of thought and were placed before us on the table. Cars materialized at the gates upon arrival, deposited their passengers, and winked quietly out of existence when they departed.

Now that we were securely isolated from the outside world—and with scarcely any remorse that I can recall—we proceeded with the sorcery.

We arrived at Booth Lodge late on a Friday night and were shown into a large warm room where we sat around on chairs, on sofas, and on the floor. Stories were handed out and we were told the reading order for the following morning. With surprise and some anxiety I found that my story was scheduled first. This initial response was followed by about twelve hours of nervousness.

Sorcery, you see, is a hard business. Done with half a heart it produces a lot of smoke and egg gas. Done seriously, and with honest spells, there is a shadowy hope of creating a living prism. This is a story; a magic, a masterpiece. But it isn't always easy. The spells have to be learned, the amalgams acquired. This requires luck, knack or a workshop. Which shows you magic in action and may make you into an arch-mage or something. But it is still hard work.

Hard . . . Work.

For days or weeks or months you have worked on a story, a magical composition. You have slept on it, and thought on it and frustrated on it, and you have finally written it. As you timidly expected, it didn't do exactly what you wanted, it was not nearly as good as you thought it might have been: but it was born of joy and mirth. And anyhow, you knew that if it came to any judgement there were always worse stories around, even published in high-paying magazines.

So what did you do with it? Why, of course, being an aspiring writer, you popped it in the post and sent it off to the workshop competition.

Now you find yourself sitting in this warm room. It is early morning. Outside it is so cold that there is frost on the glass, and as you sit there you feel your skin tingle. And the muscles on your neck contract until you can scarcely move your head. Your breathing is irregular. You are very pale-feeling. You *might* be having a baby, judging by the symptoms.

What are you doing here?

Go on, get up on your feet, and *run*.

Nobody will notice. They're more terrified than you are; they actually have to *say* something.

Why is it so hot in here? Why is it so intense? The laughter doesn't sound right. Hide, quickly: she's coming.

And Ursula comes in. She is a small thin lady, who smokes a pipe, and smiles friendly, and sits on the floor.

Introductions and occupations, age and aspirations, go round in circles. You're on first name terms now with your fellow aspirants, but what about—

Mrs. Le Guin? Ursula Le Guin? Ur—Ursula? Yes, Ursula.

"Okay," she says, "who's first bait?" Or something like that.

Me. (Timidly)

So they begin. Ursula reveals the main rule. That is, the rule of vegetable silence. Which means you have to sit like a vegetable throughout the criticisms of the others, without once speaking or replying. You can groan, and you do; sometimes, in desperation or indignation, you make vigorous head movements or hand gestures. But since you are helpless these gestures are innocently overlooked.

In the absence of anything *physical* to do you content yourself with a perennial frown and sit scrunched up on the floor between the armchair and the door.

In your lap rests a notepad and a pen and your hands fiddle with the pen. No one has yet said anything; no one has yet realized the exact nature of the criticism they must give. But this uncertainty is only temporary.

"Well, I liked the story," someone begins, "I really thought it was nice, but—"

The world ends, not with a whimper, but with a but. And continues to end, over and over, until you think it can't possibly end one more time.

Your critics have told you, in intimate details, exactly what is wrong with your story, what it is about a particular sentence that gave them a pain, why this character shouldn't have said this, and should have done that. Slowly, and kind of reluctantly, you begin to realize that writing is no longer a hobby to be done perfunctorily. You realize that for the past three or four or five years you have secretly been treating it as a hobby, not as your work. The walls have come down and you can see that to write something worthwhile is going to require an enormous portion of your self and your time. It can't be done flippantly, or casually. It's got to be a total commitment, to words, to feelings, to ideas, to people, to yourself. And to the Characters.

You learn, or you begin to suspect, that there is an esoteric logic to writing, a form or stratum that you must attain and crack before you can go on to further conquests. This is the commitment. It is very elusive; it avoids being found, but may, I hope, be stumbled upon.

Your legs are cramped, so you shift around. Criticisms are still flowing. You listen carefully to every word, hang on every phrase and snippet of advice. You can't be defensive or muddle-minded here: you can't say *anything*. Just sit, listen, mull over, analyse. In some ways, it is a relief.

In some; not all.

A few days, a few hours ago you were very pleased with that story: self-satisfied. Now, in the middle of these attacks, you are piercingly aware that it is only a portion or an ingredient of yourself that they are evaluating. Something you squeezed out of your brain or your world and dared to put down onto paper, openly, for them all to see. And then it doesn't seem so bad any more. Because you know, intuitively, that they understand, that they recognize and acknowledge the courage it took for you to write it and let them see it, see inside you. They have a similar courage, otherwise they would not be here.

And anyhow, the story could not be all bad.

But of course, it is. Good criticism becomes self-evident, once pointed out and explained. *Hell,* you say, *that's obvious.* But how could you have been so blind? All those silly errors, those inconsistencies of style and character? Where were they when you read and re-read the story? Of course: they were invisible.

And are they now visible?

Well, yes and no. They *are* becoming more visible all the time; and some, which earlier had been prime and insidious offenders, have now lost some of their craftiness, and are less adept at concealing themselves.

Is this the function of a workshop?

I don't know. I think it is a major part of it. You may have talent, or you may not, but the elusive art of discernment, of knowing what is right, efficacious, and generally correct must be counted as the middle point on the road to authorship.

And the other half? Well, if you are lucky, you have been stabbed alive.

Annis Shepherd

Duplicates

A pale figure loomed in Oldself's mind. She knew it was waiting, waiting for her to come home. She knelt, crouched over, her head pressed down into her dirt-stained lap. Her arms were stretched out, limp and exhausted, her fingers curled into the moist earth. The acrid odor of shath leaves was in her nostrils and the twilight wind cooled her sweat-drenched skin. As always, the Screaming Hour had passed all too quickly. It was the hour of release, the time each Oldself could escape her small darkened home; the time each one of them could yell if they wanted, or cry, or do anything but keep silent. Just the sound of whispering irritated her, making her long to lash out at those closest to her.

Oldself stood up awkwardly, her form like some misshapen tree in the darkening glade. She wiped her hands uncaringly on her coverall, the earth-brown marks like large frown lines across her breast. She moved down the time-worn path, her futile screams still echoing in her ears. She was aware of the hurrying forms of other Oldselfs darting amongst the trees, each one reluctantly returning to her home. Home. Her lips twisted in derision. What mockery that word had become since she had entered her Second Half, since she had become an Oldself, like her mother before her. How arrogant she had once been. Her thoughts flitted back to her First Half, to the time of her youth when laughter and love had enjoyed some meaning.

Oldself was moving swiftly now. She could take no pleasure in the trees that arched above the twisting path, for it was from them that her enemy was carved. Fear rippled through her as once again that waiting form flashed into her thoughts.

51

"Gradha. Release me from this. Let me be." Her silent wail rang clear and lonely through her body.

She wound her way down between an outcrop of rocks, bypassing the Place of Flames. She turned away lest the spirits of that fearsome place bring vengeance against her. It had been many years since she had approached that desolate spot and she prayed it would be many years more before she was taken there in death to be burned, her husband by her side.

As she passed through the now silent village and approached the door of her home, the pale figure in her mind seemed to grow and grow until she could visualize it towering over her screaming coldly, *Get away, get away.*

While she waited for her husband to return, she struggled with her fears, but was finally overcome. Defeated, she entered the room where her enemy waited.

Oldself stared at the smooth-white figure in the center of the room. The yellow light cast flickering shadows over its polished surface, the creamy wood, veined and flecked. Shuddering, she recalled the day it had been carved, the day it was handed to her husband, the last day of her marriage year. That had been her face then, her form, her laughter. She cursed it. It was her enemy and her self, and her husband loved it.

At the thought of Gradha, Oldself felt her resentment rise afresh. Arching her neck, she mouthed an anguished cry to Jard-Hi, her Protector.

Give me back my youth, so that my husband may love me. Give me back my love. The words throbbed through her like fire.

She allowed her gaze to shift up that curving form, and spat. Dreamily she watched the spittle ease its way down her facsimile's cheek. She did not dare remove the proof of this defilement, for never had an Oldself laid her hand on her Youngself. The thought terrified her.

A light sound disturbed her. Backing away, Oldself glanced sideways at the looming figure of her husband as he entered. Her heart ached with hate at the sight of his youthful frame, so firm and strong, not one whit changed since she had bedded him thirty spans ago. Once his touch had given her joy, but now it filled her with loathing, for how could eternal youth mate willingly with age? Yet his body would have to die with hers, when the time came, encased in flames, and the thought was comforting. Oldself glanced away for fear Gradha would guess her thoughts. Again her yearning for her First Half flooded her, that brief time of marvelous freedom when she had looked into this man's eyes and had seen him gaze lovingly in return.

Gradha, her mind whispered despairingly, Gradha!

Oldself watched her husband through her lowered lashes as he flung his hunt-spear to the floor and strode to Youngself, clasping the statue in an enveloping embrace. Her expression remained impassive, yet she burned with the knowledge that such motions of love were denied her. At the first hint of her waning youth, her husband had averted his gaze, never again to look upon her, and lavished all his love on this cold replica as custom decreed.

Gradha spoke at last, his glance automatically avoiding hers.

"Youngself, let Oldself bring me food."

Submitting to the traditional form of command, Oldself left. When she returned, it was not easy to look upon him. Gradha ate slowly, ignoring her. Even the lamplight could not disperse the unwholesome gloom that surrounded them, and Oldself felt her sense of hopelessness increase. Her arms, patient and motionless by her sides, ached unceasingly. She could not wait for the time of the Screaming Hour to return. She had to get out, escape—

"Youngself, let Oldself bring me cloth."

Gradha's words sent a chill through her heart for she knew what this would bring. As Oldself placed the soft worn material at his feet, she found herself trembling so that she could barely rise.

"Don't, Gradha. Not when I'm here." Her unuttered plea filled her with a dark suffocation so that her breath dragged in painfully.

Each movement of Gradha's arm as he poured the perfumed oil on her Youngself and began to polish it, each caress of his hand down its flowing surface, sent waves of exciting terror through her old, weary body. She let her fingers trace the wrinkled crevices of her face as if to share the loving motions enacted before her. Her loss released the flame of her desire and the fire of her pain, locking her whole being in one endless, silent scream.

Helplessly, Oldself saw her hand, vein-swelled and powerful, reach out into the darkness about her. Her fingers found and grasped a corn covered pestle, a rough point of reality. She did not hear her scream grow articulate nor see her arm merge with the heavy stone as she turned destroyer. She did not see Gradha's face, turned in horror. All she saw was the laughing mouth urging her on, the young face, *her* face, waiting, waiting. As Oldself watched her enemy crumble before her, she, too, felt herself collapse.

Gradha watched her sobbing form. His life had lost all meaning and that hour he died.

John Edward Clark

Lonely are the Only Ones

". . . Clay's left eye is puffed up bad. 'e can hardly see. 'e swings a wild left hook—uh, Robinson ducks moves in 'n jabs a left-right to the stomach 'n a left to the head 'n a left hook-right cross combination uh 'e's opened it Clay's left eye is bleeding the blood's streaming down 'is face 'e's blind in one eye! Robinson moves in for the kill uh Clay staggers back 'is gloves around 'is 'ead. Robinson bangs a left-right-left to the stomach—uh, Clay drops 'is guard, 'e fights back with a flurry of wild punches—God this kid's got guts—'e lashes out with a right 'n left 'n a right, but they all miss—Robinson shoots a glove into Clay's right eye, 'e crosses to the stomach, 'e flashes a left to 'is jaw, 'e rips a double hook to the body 'n 'head—'e's throwin' punches everywhere! Clay's hurt, 'e's blind, 'e's out on 'is feet. 'e throws a wild right hook—Oh oh it connected. It 'it Robinson—What a punch what a punch—'e throws another right hook to the 'ead, 'n another GOD I don't believe it. I just don't believe it uh 'e's knocked 'is 'ead off—Clay's knocked Robinson's 'ead off! Jus' look at the blood—uh, one, two, three, four, five, six, seven, eight, nine, TEN. It's all over it's all over—Clay's won by a knockout in the ninth. This must be the greatest—"

Click.

The wallscreen whitened. Jonathan Sumners drew a limp hand from the control switch beside his bed and sighed. "Androids are a bore. Life is a bore. Nothing to do but watch, and listen, and dream, and wait. God, to be young again!" Jonathan Sumners was three hundred and forty-seven years old. He was the oldest living man on Earth. And he felt it. He was also the only living man on Earth. And he felt that too.

"Lonely are the freaks and the uniques.
Lonely are the firsts and the lasts.
Lonely are the only ones."

He remembered the words from somewhere, sometime. Maybe they were his. He wondered. "What's it all about? *What* is the point? What *is* the point? What is *the* point? What is the *point?*" He chewed the words in his mouth, hoping that by accentuating different ones he could find an answer. "Life has no purpose other than living. So live!" His father had said that a long time ago. "So live!" He'd had it inscribed on his tombstone. "So live!" To the last man on Earth the words were not enough. "So live!" Whatever it was he was doing, it wasn't *living*. He didn't feel quite alive. He didn't feel quite dead. He was somewhere in between. He was in limbo. But even in limbo, there must be some purpose. Mustn't there?

He began to sing in a deep crackling voice.

"Oh I'm dreaming of a White Christmas
ba ba ba boom
ba ba ba boom..."

Wishing that he could remember more of the song, Jonathan nestled into the air bed, settled; and drooped his eyelids. The curved line on the brainwave oscilloscope flattened as he fell asleep...

The presents had all been wrapped in cellophane and laid out under a green plastic tree that flickered with tiny carnival lights.

The windows had been frosted up with white imitation snow spray and the thermostats turned low. The room had been garnered by an interior decorator with shimmering crystal ornaments and pulsating neon globes that flashed goodwill tidings. The tapedeck had been programmed only to play festive songs with a popularity quotient of 66.5 or higher.

And now the family was seated around the thermo-table, ready to enjoy a good old-fashioned Christmas dinner. Jonathan, the eldest son, had been given the honor of carving the Christmas turkey. For a nine year old, it was an awesome responsibility.

"I want a wing, no, make that a drumstick."

"*I* want a drumstick."

"Hey, I want a drumstick too."

"Well, you can't have one. Me and Martha asked first."

"Quiet children. Jon, give Bert and Martha a drumstick. Jim, you had a drumstick last Christmas. You can have a wing or some white meat."

"Aw, shucks!"

"Don't cut it too thick, Jon. It has to go around."

Jonathan shook the electric carving knife in his sweaty hand, and looked down at the small steaming bird. His lips watered. His heart pounded. He knew, he just knew, he was going to mess it all up. He felt like a doctor operating on a mortally wounded man.

"Scalpel!"

"Here."

"No, no. I want a scalpel, not a probe. Don't you know the difference between a scalpel and a probe?"

"Sorry. My mistake. Here!"

"Thank you, *nurse.*"

Slowly the surgeon-in-white edged the fire-blade into the open chest of the body on the operating table. His head ran with perspiration. His fingers stuttered. The blade cut slowly, finely, deeply. Too deeply. "Fark!" he yelped, as the artery burst open and a jet of blood squirted him in the face. He jammed his hand into the wound, like the little Dutch boy who stuck his finger in the dyke, to try to hold back the flood. But it was no use. "Sponge! Protractors! Watch the cardio support system! Keep up the lung pressure! Clamps! Jees, what a mess!" The surgeon was covered with blood. The four nurses were covered with blood. The patient was covered with blood. The table and the equipment and the floor and the walls and the ceiling were covered with blood. Everything was bright red and wet.

Suddenly the patient sat up and screamed gutlessly. His face was hideously misshapen. It was the face of Jonathan Sumners.

"Eeeoww! Arrrrr!" He ground his teeth until they cracked, and spat them out.

"Wake up! Wake up!"

"Ooooooh! Arrrrr!" Howling, Jonathan Sumners opened his eyes to a slender white-capped face.

"Wake up Jonathan. Wake up. You've been nightmaring again. Relax."

Jonathan relaxed. He focused his plastoid eye lenses on a

familiar face. It was his favorite nurse, Big Tits.

"Was it a bad one?" she asked, wiping his eyes. Water ran down the furrows in his cheeks.

"It was ba-a-a-a-a-d. This time they chopped up an artery. It was awful!" A hollow voice rasped from the sunken pit of his mouth. "These nightmares are getting worse and worse. What do they mean, Big Tits?" Her proper name was Android First Class Marilyn Monroe. But Jonathan always called her "Big Tits." When you were the last man on Earth, you could get away with anything.

"Gosh, I don't know, Jonathan. I honestly don't know," she purred, red-lippedly. "But I wouldn't worry about it. Doctor Freud will be in later for another session. He'll find out what's wrong. He'll stop those silly nightmares."

"If they keep up, I'll go mad. Mad!" he screamed. "I spend half of my life asleep. I like to dream. Dreams are one of the few things I have left. Now I'm even losing them. These nightmares are choking me. I'm afraid to close my eyes anymore. I'm afraid." He snivelled dryly and buried his face in the bed.

"Don't cry. Please don't cry," the android pleaded.

Jonathan cried.

"Please Jon. You know how I hate it when you cry." She caressed his wispy gray head with soft mechanical fingers. "Things aren't that bad. Please don't be unhappy. Please don't cry. You know I can't permit you to suffer pain."

Jonathan whimpered.

A pin-prick suddenly tingled his upper arm. He uncovered his face to see a tiny red spot swelling on the loose skin.

"Damn you! Damn you, Big Tits!" he cried. "I don't want your artificial happiness." She stood smiling, a hypodermic in her hand. "I like to cry. I *have* to cry."

"It's for your own good, Jonathan," she murmured.

"Don't tell me what's for my own good," he snapped. "What would you know, you, you, android! What do androids know about life? Now get out!"

Obediently she left.

"Damn you all. To hell with everything and everyone." Effervescent chemicals coursed through his blood. Waves of euphoria rippled outward. Jonathan glowed. He was so very happy.

He wandered his eyes along the glistening white-screen walls of his home, and sniffed. He stared unblinking at the thin pulsating purple tubes that fed from the machines deep within his wrinkled body, and giggled. He watched the ceaseless light rhythms of the blood pumps and oxygen pumps and nutrient pumps and faecal pumps that crowded around his bed, and laughed.

"This room is me," he shouted. "This room with all its stupid machines *is* me. I can see my guts. I can see my guts throbbing around me. It's so funny, so funny. The last man on Earth. Ha! I'm a prisoner, and I can't escape. A room can't escape from a room? He laughed tears. He cried joy. Convulsed, he reached for the control switch.

Click.

The screen shimmered alive in full tri-di color.

Like a goddess she rose dripping wet from the sea. Her born body glistened beneath a white robe that clung transparent to her skin. The icy white waves caressed her lovingly. She dug a foot into the soft sand, threw back a seaweed tangle of blonde hair proudly, and smiled at the camera. Her legs were long and slender, with firm supple thighs that held the secret of life. Her waist was small and delicately shaped, like a priceless Grecian vase. Her breasts were of sculptured marble, full and rounded, with pink nipples that tempted like strawberry creams. Her face was glowing sunshine. Her lips were fiery embers. Her eyes were diamond studded stars. Her name was Athena.

Panting softly, like a purring kitten, she knelt down upon the sands, brushed the saltwater from her lips, and ran fingers through flaxen strands of hair. A whispering breeze kissed her face, and murmuring sounds pricked her ears. Looking up instinctively, she saw him.

He stood naked before her, muscles rippling across his body like trout through still waters. God, he was beautiful! His legs were massive auburn tree trunks, and as he moved them the earth trembled. His matted chest was as broad as a bullock's, and glistening with oil. His arms were steel thick sinews, with rugged biceps that bulged like weathered granite boulders. His face was cast bronze. His face was the face of Jonathan Sumners from long ago.

He smiled. As he stepped into the moonlight, her eyes stilled at the sight of the cobra that had reared angrily between his thighs. She stood and, tearing the robe from her body, she ran toward him, and fell at his feet. Her warm fingers stroked him wetly. She parted her glowing lips and caressed him with a fiery soft tongue that made him throb. He reached down and cupped her heaving breasts in his calloused hands. She sighed heatedly and fell to the sand, spreading her legs wide, inviting joyous oblivion.

Exhaling fire, he mounted her.

Like a barbarian battering at the gates of Rome, he rammed deep inside her, killing her with joy. Her face was bursting, exploding with fire. A Krakatoan eruption was coming; you could see it in her eyes. The shockwaves made her tremble. She gulped air, and dug her fingers into the muscles of his back.

"Vomit!" Jonathan Sumners commanded.

As their fiery lips met in a sea of ecstasy, the lovers covered each other's bodies in pale, synthetic vomit.

Jonathan Sumners laughed, and laughed, and laughed. He rocked in his bed. Tears ran from his eyes, dribbled from the folds in his mouth.

"God what a joke. What a cruel joke," he gulped, wheezing laughter. "All the world's a stage, and all the people ha ha merely androids. Christ it's funny. I feel sick, ha, ha. Earth's a refrigerator, a frozen world, a giant television studio. And me, why I'm the director. Yes, I'm the Cecil B. de Mille of the Milky Way. No, no. I'm more than that, much more. Why, I'm God! Yes, I'm God. God, I must be God!" he cried out. "Let there be light and cameras and action!"

Jonathan grabbed his controls and spun the dial randomly to another remote control camera. There were millions of them positioned throughout the Earth.

A voice interrupted him.

"I'm dying, Jon. I can feel it. I'm dying of boredom."

He looked across at the adjacent bed, into the sallow face of his friend, Miles Fargo.

"Don't say that, Miles. You're all I have left. You and me, we got to stick together. The last two men on Earth got to stick together."

"I can't keep up the pretense. There's just no sense. There's no reason anymore." Jon had heard the words before, but this time they seemed strangely final.

"Hope, Miles," his voice wavered. "As long as we're alive we can hope. You ever wonder why we're the only ones to survive the Great Plague? I do. Maybe it's God's will."

"I don't believe in God, Jon. But I do believe in the Devil!" Miles curled his lips in a demonic smile.

"We're the last two human beings. We owe it to humanity to survive." Jonathan wagged a finger in the air and tried hard to convince himself.

"I owe humanity nothing, Jon. Nothing. Look at me. I'm a prisoner. All my guts have been eaten away." He pinched the white sheet that covered his body, tapped the silver throat mike in his neck. "I can't do anything anymore. I can't enjoy a good meal. Or a good wine. Or a good woman. I can't even enjoy a good piss. All I can do is lie here, and talk, and sleep, and watch that bloody screen." His face seemed to sink, accentuating all the sagging lines.

"Years ago, Miles, there were millions of people who did nothing all day but sleep and watch tiny television monitors. They were healthy. They could have done anything they wanted to. They chose to watch the monitors. They must have been happy."

"They probably all died of boredom."

"Don't give up, Miles. Please, don't give up."

"Goodbye, Jonathan."

Miles Fargo closed his eyes.

Jonathan cried as he watched the funeral march on the screen. The entire android population, some seven billion strong, crowded for a thousand miles along the streets. It was the biggest cast he'd ever seen, in the biggest production he'd ever seen. There were weeping android men, and women, and children. Even the android dogs and cats seemed sad. Synthetic tears gushed down white gutters.

Jonathan closed his eyes.

"Blood, blood, blood. We need more blood."

"How much?"

"Buckets and buckets. Increase the flow to 3.5 fpm's. Quickly!"

Looking up, Jonathan saw the surgeon-in-white, who reached his red hands deep down into a hole in his chest, and probed around. He grabbed hold of something. Slowly he lifted it out, dripping. It squished. It squirmed. It throbbed red. It was a bleeding heart.

"I've found the problem. It's defective. There's a puncture. We'll have to replace it."

The surgeon fingered the swelling arteries and veins. He gently massaged the outer walls of the left auricle and ventricle. The heart swam around in his hands.

"Damn thing's as slippery as an egg yolk," he said. And then he dropped it on the floor. "Oops!"

Jonathan screamed, and screamed, and screamed. He blew his eyelids open. He jolted himself awake.

But the surgeon-in-white was still there, bending over him, menacing him. He would not go away.

"Get away from me you butcher!" Jonathan cried hoarsely, clawing the air. "Get away!"

"Relax, Jon, relax. It's only me."

As Jonathan's lenses came back into focus, he relaxed. The surgeon-in-white was gone. Only Dr. Sigmund Freud stood over him.

"Hel-lo Shithead," Jonathan greeted his bearded friend. The words fell cracked from his wet lips.

"Hello, Jon. Another bad dream, eh? Well, it's all over now. You can relax." Dr. Freud's voice had a magical, soothing quality. Jonathan felt it flow over him, healing him. He calmed down.

"Another *nightmare*. They're getting worse. What do they mean? What in hell do they mean?" He stared into the android's smoothly sculptured face.

"I've told you before, Jon. They're only a reaction to your situation. You're a sick man. You're surrounded by medical equipment, and doctors, and nurses. It's only natural you should dream about familiar things."

"No!" Jonathan was emphatic. "These nightmares mean more than that. There's something wrong. It's on the tip of my mind. If only I could remember." He wrinkled his balding eyebrows.

"Nonsense," chided Dr. Freud, softly.

"You're holding something back from me, aren't you, Doc?"

"No—why should I?"

Jonathan looked up at the android and fancied he could detect a hint of deception in the expressionless face. Cold, still eyes stared at him from behind gentle tanned features. He almost hated him. What the hell was an android doing with a tan, anyway?

"Stick your finger up your nose when you say that, Shithead," he snapped angrily.

Obediently, the android stuck his left index finger up his left nostril, and repeated, "No—why should I?"

Jonathan cried drily. His loneliness struck him like a blade in the back. He was alone. That wasn't a doctor he was talking to. That was only a . . . a . . . Shithead.

"I can't take anymore. I want out. Let me die like a man!" he cried.

"You know that's impossible," replied Dr. Freud, nasally.

"But there's just no sense, no reason anymore. I'm all alone." Jonathan's voice echoed hollowly off the walls.

"I could send Bertrand Russell in to talk with you, if you like. Or Aristotle. Or Karl Marx. Or Adolph Hitler. Or anyone." The doctor smiled hopefully.

"They're bloody androids!" snorted Jonathan. "I want to talk to people."

"You know that's impossible."

"Then let me die!"

"You know that's impossible."

"Kill me!"

"You know that's impossible, impossible, impossible . . ." The android's larynx froze. His left index finger had short-circuited his vocal system. Yet still he stood there, like a silly parrot, squawking, ". . . impossible, impossible, impossible . . ."

"Get out!" spat Jonathan.

Obediently Dr. Freud left, spluttering.

Jonathan turned his heavy head to one side, and posed a riddle. "When is a man not a man?" He'd always thought the answer was, "When he can't live like a man." Now he knew the answer really was, "When he can't die like a man."

He closed his eyes and prayed that they would not open again. Darkness.

Bright white light shot at him. It burnt through his eyelids. Slowly he slid them open, and squinted. Everything was white. The ceiling was white. The walls were white. The machines were white. The bed was white. Everything was white. A pair of white hands with wriggling white fingers reached down for him. It was the surgeon-in-white. Jonathan snapped his eyelids shut, and trembled. He could feel hands grabbing at his head.

"Vich way? Is it zis vay? Or zis vay?" someone asked in a gruelling German accent.

"Careful you don't break his neck."

"My dear boy, Doktor Frankenstein never makes ze mistake!"

Jonathan's head was jerked violently from side to side, up and down, round and around. He reeled. He felt dizzy. He choked. He was being strangled. He opened his eyes and tried desperately to adjust to the light.

He saw himself, and screamed.

He saw a headless corpse on the operating table, and screamed. He saw a head, his head, under a white arm, and screamed. And screamed, and screamed, and screamed.

His mouth cracked apart. His eyelids flickered. The surgeon-in-white did not let go. The dream would not dissolve. Like an ancient pearl diver who had gone too deep, he knew he would never reach the surface again. But still he had to try. His lungs aflame, he clawed at the water, higher and higher. And suddenly its icy fingers released him. He broke through to the air. He woke up gulping.

Dr. Sigmund Freud stood over him, an empty hypodermic in his white hand.

"I can't take anymore!" Jonathan wailed. "If you won't kill me, then these nightmares will. I'm going mad. If only I knew what they meant."

Dr. Freud's face had an illusion of sympathy. Quite unexpectedly, he bent down and said, "Okay Jonathan. There seems no alternative. I'll tell you."

Jonathan looked up apprehensively. He was surprised. For months he'd asked the question. Was he about to be answered now? He trembled.

"The simple truth, Jonathan, is that you're not the last man on Earth."

"What?" He couldn't believe it. "You mean there's someone else? Others? Where? Why wasn't I. . .?"

"No, no, Jonathan. You misunderstand." Dr. Freud's voice

softened. "Miles Fargo was the last man on Earth. You're..."

"But Miles died years ago. And I'm still alive."

"You're an android, Jonathan."

Jonathan said, did, nothing. Then:

"Ha, ha—big joke! Take a look at me! Look at this rotten body! Look at all these machines around me, and tell me I'm an android!"

Doctor Freud looked down at him, looked around at the machines, and repeated, "You're an android, Jonathan." He spoke slowly. "You were constructed and programmed exactly one hundred and forty-seven years ago to keep Miles Fargo company. You're the most complex android ever produced. We used an experimental synthetic human brain in you. We found it in a glass jar in an old laboratory. But you're still only an android."

The words should have fallen on him like a death blow. They should have suffocated him. But they didn't. Maybe he really was an android. Maybe in the back of his mind he'd always known. Yes it all made sense now. The nightmares were memories. He remembered the surgeon-in-white, the nurses. They weren't pulling him apart. They were putting him together!

"But why? If I'm an android, what am I doing here?"

Dr. Freud moved towards him and held his hand, machine to machine. "Just before he died, we told Miles about you. He didn't seem angry. He smiled strangely and said, 'Take care of him. Take good care of Jonathan.' And we have. You're the only reason we all still exist."

Jonathan's eyes filled with tears. Some inner safety valve had released them. He cried with joy. At last he had found a purpose for his existence. It was a strange purpose, but it was a purpose: he was God to a bunch of androids! He was the reason for their existence, and they were the reason for his.

His scarred lips curled into a smile. He laughed—and somehow it was a relief. He wasn't a man. He *wasn't* a man. He knew that now. But he knew something else: he knew he wasn't an android either. Years of brooding had somehow changed him. He wasn't a man, and he wasn't an android. He was something in between. He was somewhere in limbo. Suddenly he remembered the words Miles Fargo had told him seconds before he died. Miles was right. Old Miles had known what it was all about.

"Lonely are the freaks and the uniques.
Lonely are the firsts and the lasts.
Lonely are the only ones."

I never began by writing short stories. When I set out to become a writer, I decided to write a novel. That was in the summer of 1970. The novel was written on both sides of foolscap paper—not ordinary foolscap, mind you: it was green, pink, red and yellow. I can well imagine what the secretary at Angus and Robertson must have thought when I handed her my treasure. Needless to say, it was soon returned to me. Undaunted, I rewrote the novel and began my great crusade around Melbourne looking for a sympathetic publisher. The only encouragement I received was from one in North Melbourne: they said they would like to publish it but they did not think it would make any money...

In subsequent years, I wrote some short stories—mainly to prove to myself that it could be done. I sent them out to the American magazines. They sent them back. Later on in life I learned that I could live with rejection slips. Then, in 1974, the Australian SF Convention ran a small writers' workshop and I had the dubious honor of reading aloud what I had written to other people. Man, I died a thousand deaths! But I learned.

STEFAN VUCAK

In 1974 I attended the Convention writers' workshop organized by Lee Harding, for which I had written my first sf story. Virginia Woolf has said that "Literature is strewn with the wreckage of men who have minded beyond reason the opinions of others." This may be so, but thank heavens I listened when Lee said my writing was "too pretty." It took me a year of tormenting doubt before I understood and appreciated what he meant—by which time I was ready to attempt writing another short story—this time for Ursula's workshop...

ANNIS SHEPHERD

Pip Maddern

The Ins and Outs of The Hadhya City-State

One of the theories about the Hadhya people was that they were the "victims of a very severe Ice Age which had manifested itself when their culture and technology were at a sufficiently advanced level of development to enable the formation of a culturally viable troglodyte society."

As I came to know the Hadhya a little, partly through observation and partly from Marten's diaries, that theory made more and more sense to me, despite its pretentious terminology. For where else but in caves could the Hadhya have learned to love all things dim, claustrophobic and intricate? Where else could they have learnt to live at the same time close to their neighbors physically and remote from them spiritually? Where else had they learned to see in the dark?

For the Hadhya were nocturnal more strictly than Terrans now are diurnal. They lived and worked and saw entirely by night. If forced to go out in the daytime, they donned thick dark goggles with the defiant courage of an ancient Terran miner putting on his lamp helmet. Daylight was a symbol to them of all that was bright, brash, and over-obvious; to a man, they deprecated it.

It made it very hard for me to pick one Hadhya from another— even in the case of Sulen, with whom I worked night after night on the problem of Marten's disappearance. To me, peering through the gloom, they all looked alike—small, stocky and precise, like little wooden dolls, with smooth, round pale faces, and subdued, discreet voices.

And of course I never learned my way about the city-state. There were no street-lights with the Hadhya, and no straight roads either. I had no hope of finding my way with only a torch to light me through the queer, circling streets that always led to something unexpected—markets merging into stately gardens, subtle with night-scented flowers, shopping streets debouching into grain-crops, which in turn somehow led to palaces, or music rooms; or back to markets again. So I did not go out unless one of the Hadhya escorted me. Fortunately, I have never suffered from claustrophobia; otherwise the dark, and the winding high-walled streets, and my small gloomy room would have driven me almost to breaking point. All in all, it did not surprise me that Marten could have lost himself in the city-state. The problem was, how had the Hadhya lost him?

For the city-state was closely settled, and extended for miles. I did not see how he could go unseen in it. And he could never be mistaken for one of the Hadhya; he was a good six inches taller than the average, his skin was dark, and he was comparatively blind in the night. The Hadhya had a good system of radio communications throughout the city-state, which they regularly used for the transfer of all sorts of gossip. So why had Marten not been discovered?

I had first to dispose of the tentative theory that had permeated the Department, that the Hadhya had murdered Marten, and were concealing the fact. For why, in that case, had they troubled to report the matter to headquarters, and ask for help? The more I knew the Hadhya, the worse stumbling-block this appeared to the murder theory. To communicate with Terra, the Hadhya had had to use Marten's instantaneous transmitter. The Hadhya set an enormous value on self-sufficiency, both personal and racial. To be forced to call another planet for help, and have to use that planet's technology to do so, was such a deadly humiliation that they never told me who had sent the message. Sulen talked to him as "a friend." I knew enough of Hadhya language forms to know that this could have meant "an acquaintance," "a stranger," or "myself"—and that the vagueness was intentional. So I asked no further, though I often wished I knew whose goodwill had successsfully fought it out with his pride. But that it was a message of goodwill, I was certain. The Hadhya would not have humiliated themselves to boast of murder.

But Marten might still be dead. I nearly came to the conclusion that he was—say through his own error and folly—and that the Hadhya were tactfully refraining from saying so. But this did not accord with the Hadhya attitude to death, which was realistic and open in the extreme. They had, of course, metaphors and paraphrases for the word "death" (as, indeed, they had for almost anything); but they did not use them in talking of Marten. Furthermore, funerals were important social occasions to the Hadhya, eagerly anticipated, and remembered in loving detail. I felt sure that if Marten had died, they would have held a suitable funeral for him as soon as I arrived.

So where was Marten? I could not go out myself and look for him with any efficiency. I could not send for the police, since the Hadhya had none (though they had a very complex system of law courts, and took enormous interest in details of legal precedent and equity, quite beyond my grasp of either law or Hadhya language). I could, and did, sit night after night reading Marten's diaries for some clue as to where he had gone, or trying to elicit from Sulen, through a fog of half-understood language and metaphor, a statement of the places where Marten might be.

The whole thing was slowed down by the elaborate courtesy of the Hadhya. Sulen considered it ill-bred to correct my mistakes by anything but the most obscure and distant inference. And he never once started a conversation with me without discussing in most intricate detail the weather, the skies, and the prospects of rain. That was Hadhya etiquette. I took pains to learn some of the right responses, and was awarded Sulen's grave approval.

"Earth-gold mourns the absence of her lover, Sky-silver," he would observe seriously.

"She will not enter our homes without him," I would reply equally seriously.

"Let him descend from the mountains, and we shall yet welcome them," he would finish, inclining his head approvingly.

Perhaps it is a tiresomely long-winded way of saying that the crops need rain, and that the harvest will be poor without it. But I think now that I shall always be nostalgic for those long, gentle conversations with Sulen sitting still and quiet in the gloom across the table from me.

In reading Marten's diary, I saw how careful I must be in talking to Sulen. For it was plain that Marten, through no fault of his own, had lost the respect of the Hadhya, and that consequently his work had suffered. It appeared that one of the Hadhya had one night asked him about the small emergency transmitter he carried. It was

quite standard equipment among us, meant only to transmit an
S.O.S. to an orbiting space craft in case of desperate need. Marten
explained this, and instantly dropped thirty points in Hadhya
estimation. In times of danger, the Hadhya revered self-sufficiency,
or at the very least, group solidarity. They would willingly have died
rather than be dependent on a technological cry for help. Thinking to
recoup his loss of prestige Marten let it be known that he had ceased
to carry his transmitter. That, he found, was an even worse move. The
Hadhya admitted (sadly) that some, such as the very young or the
very sick, were not self-sufficient. Their business was to admit it
humbly, and strive, over a long period, to become so. If Marten were
so weak as to need his transmitter, possibly he would learn better in
time. But he would not learn by throwing it away, and saying he did
not need it, when everyone could see that he was not changed in the
least.

From that moment on, Marten wrote, the Hadhya patronized
him. They would give him words for his vocabulary lists, and scraps
of information, but anything he really wanted to know was met with a
gentle "I think the visitor does not yet hear this matter with me."
"Hear" was one Hadhya word for "understand"; but it meant
"understand" in the simplest sense—to know the gist of something, to
have a general or superficial acquaintance with it, as a child, or even
an animal, might understand. The word for complete adult
comprehension was to "wind through" something—like a person
mastering a maze. Therefore Marten would have been overjoyed even
to have been told that he did not "wind through" something. Yet the
Hadhya were not being unkind; he recognized that. They were not
even doing what they thought best for him—only what they would
have wished to have been done to them, had they behaved in a similar
childish fashion.

But I, more fortunate than Marten, could use his experiences as
a guide, and fared better correspondingly. One night Sulen even
offered to take me to the Hadhya equivalent of a concert. It was held
in the open air; the musicians sat as far apart as possible with their
backs to each other; and they all played different tunes on different
instruments at the same time for a long time. But I was glad to have
gone, not only for the weird, soft music, but for Sulen's moderate
comment afterwards—"I think the visitor may yet wind through with

us the unliving voices." I was by no means sure that I would even understand the music, but I was overwhelmingly glad that Sulen thought I might.

But all this got me no nearer to Marten.

I asked Sulen about the city-state—how big it was, how many roads it had, where one could walk, and so on. Some of the answers were simple; some I found incomprehensible. For example, Sulen knew precisely the area of the city-state, and the length of its walls. But when I asked about the roads, I was told firmly that there was only one road in the city-state. This seemed so odd, that I wasted two nights checking exhaustively my definitions of "road" and "one"; but they were correct, and seemed complete. Then I tried to introduce the concept of various types of road-system—arterial, grid-pattern, spiral, and so on. Sulen was interested in the spiral, and gave me the Hadhya word for it; but he intimated gently that it was not what he meant by the one road. I thought he hinted that I had not gone far enough, and spent hours drawing for him complex interlocking multi-branched spirals that would have done credit to an ancient Irish manuscript. Sulen liked my more complicated efforts; but none of them reminded him of the road. He seemed to think it a kind of game—as if I knew the answer all the time, and was politely circumlocuting. For fear of disillusioning him, I gave it up.

I went back and read Marten's diaries again. This time what struck me was his utter misery. We were all used to loneliness, but he was desperately lonely. The Hadhya, in all kindness, treated him like the child they thought him to be. Their reasons were too complex to explain to the Department in his few minutes' transmission daily. The Hadhya did not offer to take him out—they thought he would not "hear" anything they showed him, and that he needed the time to reflect on his shortcomings, and learn patience and wisdom. They came and talked to him at odd moments about things he did not want to hear. Left, apart from this, to his four walls and the dark, he felt as if he were in a prison. He dared not go out by day lest he should lose caste still more with the Hadhya; so he went out by himself, at night, repeatedly, and got lost repeatedly, and had to be escorted home. Each time, the Hadhya told him kindly not to do it again until he had learned to "hear" and "wind through." No doubt they thought him a very slow pupil. In the end he went out and did not come back.

It made me wonder if he had committed suicide. But there was still the problem of how he could have hidden his body from the Hadhya to be solved in that case. And by what means could he have killed himself? Cultural ambassadors were forbidden to carry weapons or dangerous drugs; the Hadhya did not use knives at meal-times; and it would have been beyond me to find myself a rope to hang myself or a pond to drown myself in the city-state. And I had better chances than Marten had had.

What if he had tried to get out of the city-state altogether? I had not considered this possibility because it seemed such a senseless thing to do; preliminary surveys had shown almost all the planet to be bleak and rocky, the Hadhya subsisting only with much ingenious diligence in their intensely cultivated city-state. But Marten, I knew, had been a lover of wilderness and rough country; he might have grown so tired and sick of the ordered Hadhya territory, with its smooth, high walls that even a desert seemed to offer a pleasant change. There was a small note cramped in at the bottom of one of his diary pages—"There are too many walls in this country, and not enough gates." I decided to ask Sulen if Marten could have left the city-state without anyone seeing him go, though I still could not see how he would have found his way out.

It was difficult to ask. I had to be blunter than usual, for time was running out. I had been three and a half weeks in the Hadhya city-state already. I knew Marten had had his seven days' emergency rations on him when he left; but if he were lost in the desert, even if he had found water to drink, he would have to come in soon or starve. An alien wilderness is no place to forage in. Sulen was uneasy at my plain-speaking; his answers became, if anything, briefer and more obscure than before.

I asked Sulen if Marten could be in the desert surrounding the city-state. Apparently, the idea struck him as ridiculous. He said (in brief), that the desert was too far away, miles from Marten's room; it was a hard journey; no-one ever went there; Marten would have to be a bird to go; and much more to the same effect. I can still see the pale disc of his face as he turned almost impatiently to me, and said "The first visitor—I do not think he is a snake, to slip through walls, or a leaf, to fly over them. How will he travel to the desert?"

I asked about the gates to the city-state. Sulen seemed struck dumb. He said, at last, with desperate tolerance, "I think you do not wind through with me—there are no wall-breaks in our world."

"But the first visitor could perhaps climb the walls," I suggested diffidently.

Even in the dusk I could see the despairing lift of Sulen's eyebrows—an expression he wore only when I, by being exceptionally obtuse, had forced him to be comparatively blunt. He said, with an immense effort, "Is he a man? Do men climb walls?"

I was silent.

Slowly, Sulen's brows returned to their normal level. Still more slowly, a slight crease gathered between them. I think he was remembering that Marten had not, in other ways, behaved like what the Hadhya called a man. He said, almost uncertainly, "But perhaps the visitors do things we would not wind through."

I still said nothing. He continued, "Perhaps the visitors climb walls on their own jewel-in-the-sky."

I said that Terrans did sometimes climb walls on their own planet. Sulen's eyes opened wide with concentration. He sat for several minutes like that, apparently thinking furiously. I took the risk of prompting him gently.

"But the first visitor will not be in the desert. You said it is a long way outside, I think?"

Sulen's eyebrows rose again. "No," he said, almost hurriedly. "No, you do not yet wind through with me. It is a short way outside."

Very gently, I put down my pen, with which I had been taking notes. I waited until I could command the exasperation in my voice. I said, "But you said that the desert is a long way away, and the city-state many miles in length and breadth."

"Yes," said Sulen.

"Then it is a long way outside."

"No," said Sulen.

"It is a long way to the desert which is around the city-state, but it is a short way outside?"

"Yes," said Sulen.

"The desert is outside the city-state?"

"Yes," said Sulen.

We sat and stared at each other. I saw in front of me nights and nights of work, checking over again all the Hadyha meanings and

metaphors for "desert," for "outside," for "journey," for "city-state."
I did not have much time. Marten would be dead while I conned my
vocabulary lists, while Sulen and I sat one each side of the table, both
knowing that I did not understand what was plain to him, I unable to
ask the right question, he unable to give me clearer answers than he
had done already.

We sat and looked at each other.

After a long while, Sulen took out his cat's cradle string. The
Hadhya considered cat's cradle a form of discipline or meditation and
would spend hours concentrating on forming and dissolving intricate
thread patterns. I hope it inspires him to something within the next
few days, I thought bitterly, watching Sulen.

But he was not looping the string around his fingers. Instead, he
laid it out on the table in the form of a circle.

Watching me out of the corners of his eyes to see that I was
observing him, he then drew the circle into a long, thin oval, thus:

Finally, and more slowly than I would have believed possible, he
wound the oval into a spiral, thus:

He said the word for spiral, and the word for road, tracing his
finger down the middle of the loop. Then he turned his back to me,
and hid his face in his hands.

I bent over the table-top and saw the whole thing clear.

The string was the unbroken wall of the city, the table-top the
desert; inside the loop Sulen and I sat and talked endlessly over the
crops, and the rain and the meanings of words; outside the loop, but
inside the spiral, Marten wandered endlessly, trying to find the place
where he had managed to climb the wall. Or did he? Was there water
on the outside of the walls?

I asked Sulen. He did not turn round, and his voice drifted
mournfully over his shoulder.

"Men do not climb the walls. I do not know from seeing. But it is told that Elende, who raised the city-state, gouged great trenches outside the walls for stone, and that water sprang in the bare rock. You see, it is a balance to the inside; it is light and wet and lifeless. Inside is dark, and men till the dry earth."

Marten might be alive then. I would have to send an urgent message to the Department, get them to send a hovering craft with an infra-red scanner, to find him if he were alive, and men to seek his body if he were dead. I wished him dead. I wished him killed in the fall from the wall, before he knew that he had escaped only into a worse prison. I wished him drowned in a rock-pool before he had time to starve slowly to death in a high-walled trench of a maze, before he could lose his strength stumbling among the rocks, and his breath shouting to the echoing walls. I wished him dead, and out of hell.

My department is very keen on the promotion of goodwill among planets. It is the subject of numerous pep-talks to all the staff. Instances are quoted where lives and money and prestige have been semi-miraculously saved through the goodwill engendered and sedulously fostered by the departmental experts. Marten had goodwill to the Hadya, and they to him; and me to him, and him to me, and they to me, and I to them. We were a positive trinity of goodwill. Yet Marten is very probably dead; and Sulen sits with his face in his hands, grieving for the pride he has sacrificed to goodwill; and I sit and wonder whether, having failed to prevent it, we can manage to make good Marten's death and the loss of Sulen's self-respect.

Edward Mundie

The Gift

It was dark when I awoke; black with glimmerless blackness that defied the very thought of sight.

I found myself strange to myself; no wonder at that. I mused a little on the others. Was I the first of them, the first to wake?

I moved my limbs, hands creaked as they extended, fingers flexed protestingly and drily brushed strange surfaces with just a hint of feeling. Pain was there, of course, an agony in every movement, but I welcomed every pang, bringing as it did its message of returning life.

I turned a little sideways, levered myself up out of the box onto my elbow. There was so little space. Small things packed carefully beside my body tumbled down beneath me. My searching fingers, numbed yet touched with fire, explored the space and found the little store of grain. New agonies explored my vitals as tongue, jaws and stomach resumed their proper role. Thirst burst upon me. There was no water, but I found the precious oils placed nearby for this need. No pleasure came from this, for disuse had made every action of my body painful. I lay and flexed each muscle and sinew I could conceive. Hours passed in this way, but I knew that hours signified nothing, except in relation to my new strength, and the task before me.

At last the sense of well-being the wise men had predicted was upon me. My body spoke readiness, and I began the first of my new tasks, this the most important one of all, the one which carried death as the penalty of failure.

I turned in the bed. I slowly raised my shoulders against the stone canopy above, and began to lift. I brought my knees under me, braced wide, applied power with thighs, biceps, back and stomach. There was no hint of surrender in the mass above. Panic fought its way

through my veins, pounded the blood in my temples. I bunched
sinews and muscles, forced myself frenziedly at the weight above. I
thought of thousands of tons of masonry, acres of sand-drift, up-
thrown masses of land and rock torn from the core of the planet,
sealing me in these black depths.

Once more—and then again. I rested, terrified, with beating
heart. I gathered every resource of body, applied my mental powers
to assist, arranged my legs and back and thighs for every ounce of
purchase. Then up I thrust with all the straining desperation a man
will find when failure calls a price he will not pay.

And the lid moved!

I heaved again, obliquely. I felt the stone slab slide a little.
Again...and a lightning dart struck across my head with furious
intensity. I flinched against the further wall with a croak of fear; yes, it
was my first articulate sound. It was a sound that changed to a prayer
of thankfulness as my numb senses recognized the dart as a sliver of
gray daylight; my first reunion with the light of a sun I had farewelled
so long ago.

Minutes later I crawled with thudding heart and sweating brow
over the lip of my stone bed and stood erect within the chamber.
Could it be the same? Dim memory projected an image of rich drapes,
rock shapes alive with a mass of color, burning with the flickering
warmth of a score of tapers. Thus it must have been as I was laid
within the tomb, but now it was a decayed and gray cavern, a ruin of
olden times, a hole in a heap of rubble. Daylight there was, but only a
glimmer, filtering down from a chink high above. I rested, dozing a
little, thoughts bridging the ages of darkness. I remembered the
cluster of doctors, of wise men, family and faithful servants, all
gathered at my bedside during that great ceremonial.

"We prepare the way for you, O Mighty One," they had said.
"We make your pathway safe, your mission sure, your revival
awaited."

Meager words to comfort a man losing family and friends, and
everything of life.

But I must not dwell upon this.

I ate from my small store of grain, quaffed the last of the precious
oils, and inspected the door to the main corridor. It was sealed with
the waste of centuries, fused to its rock wall with a nigh unbreakable

bond of dust and clay. I picked up a bar and attacked the rock that surrounded the ancient slab. Glad indeed was I to feel the bar, that rusted remnant of fine tooling, bite at the sick old rock. Hours of work, yes, but hours only to work that great door free of its setting . . . to gain entry to the main corridor. Not too soon, because the first minutes of the sickness were upon me as I staggered down that rotten pathway, and I knew that the wise men were not truly as certain as their predictions had seemed.

The stately garb meant to gain me kingly entrance to this new and needful world had rent and fallen from me as dust. The vital strength which had flooded me was waste from my trial, and I stepped the stairway to the outer air with no liking to the great King of the 5th Dynasty, re-awakened from three thousand years of slumber.

The sun, that burning, broiling orb struck suddenly upon me. I tottered, weak and exhausted, upon the stone lip that led down to the vineyard below, and as I did, I heard exclamations in a strange tongue. I heard the clatter of feet approaching up the stones, but my dim eyes could not see in this new and savage glare, and I staggered and fell before them.

So strange and darksome this now seems, as I look back on it across the cloudy years. What paths my ill-directed feet embraced, before the fetters and the strictures of a newer world enjoined me how and what to say and do.

A lucky time it was for me, this time of waking, because the sweetly tempered seasons had yielded bounty from the earth, and vineyards sagged, and crops heavy with grain rejoiced their owners. There was food to spare for strangers. The farmers took me in, and rested me, and fed me well. Dark eyes embraced me in a puzzle, and words peered at my ears in a flood from which I gained no hint of meaning. Like some babe in crib I was forced to lie and listen, and sit to meal, and drag my steps into the sun, and presently to hoe and dig among the crops to earn the bread I ate. Words flowed across me, and one by one I took and fitted them.

But what impatience must have shown, as knife and cup and stone came haltingly alive in sound, yet worlds and marvels waited in the distance for my comprehension.

Thus a courier across infinity, with vested task to guide and mentor to a youngster world, bound to a cabbage in a hill garden.

I pass but briefly across these times of learning. The hill dialect, the meeting with the men from ships, where creaking stay and billowing sail have long replaced the sweeping oars of slaves. The journey with them to the busy continent where modern marvels oust the arts of olden time. To walk wide-eyed where coach and horses clatter in the streets. To join the throng where mouths make sounds whose tongues belong to all the ends of earth. To see the changing form of stone and brick, to see cut fingers of sappy wood set up to span house walls, and people trust themselves to tread upon floor of vegetable without a thought of danger.

Sad to see so much of culture gone without a trace. Doctors pursing lips in mock of wisdom, and wielding cruel knife without direction. The let of sorely needed blood to cure the sick. The ill-chosen herb and drug applied so rudely.

No more the cunning needles quietly slipped through skin to ragged nerve. No more the living atom set to course the blood and battle cruel invader. Lost, that power of mind where matter moved as men directed. An age of blind attempt, of ragged childishness, of clumsy endeavor.

And in the halls of Government, dismay rose up before me like some fog. Neighboring peoples railed against each other with misunderstanding, and set a mass of armies one against the other to prove the might of whim. Courts of law dispensing cruelty draped the acts with solemn robes of justice.

But these days brimmed with interest and instruction. I learned to read and write in the most common of the tongues, and prepared to make my purpose known. I would reveal the miracle of the tombs, and declare my debt to this new age. I would sit in the center of this raw and youthful world, at the right hand of Kings and Empires, and offer them the wisdom and the arts so sadly lost across the centuries.

In Germany first I confided the secret of my coming.

"A strange story and wonderful," the Chamberlain said at me, and his eyes were very wide.

"It is enjoined of me to pass this knowledge," I confided. "Not to assume any power of Government, or to usurp the Rule of State, but to sit beside the Leaders and bestow the wisdoms of my time, wherever they be seen to benefit."

"So very kind," the Chamberlain said vaguely, and his eyes were seeking past my shoulder. "Hold yourself in readiness, Good Sir, and we will send for you."

A lackey went with me to the outer door, and I observed the Chamberlain in hurry disappear, no doubt to rush the great news to his King.

But though I sat for sixty days in waiting, no summons came.

In France the story moved much in rhyme.

"Audience with the King?" they said. "Who introduces you to Court?" The ways of men are cluttered, stupid ways, but I am patient of delay, and I must learn. With blandishments and honeyed words I courted the nobility, and won my way to sit at the knee of the scented Monarch.

"You are fun," he told me in great delight.

"I learn of wit, your Highness," I enjoined him. "But the purpose here is not of entertainment, but to assist with light wherever darkness clouds the ways of men."

"My Court must hear your story. It will delight them."

"And then?" I asked.

He leaned to me confidingly. "We are generous with our friends. You shall please the Court with your tales, and there will be good coin in your fist to mark of it."

Sadly from that place I went to that old city where the great clock confides its hour in ringing majesty, and tided waters move somber and cold to the near ocean. A man of Parliament I chose to assist me. He was a good man, but in his eyes the familiar alarm crept swiftly.

"Let me tell you of that time," I said to him. I let my thoughts run on, of guided happy people, of unlocked doors of science where pain was hushed, where knowledge looked into the heart, and bodies took within a fine correction that stilled the path of their decay.

I talked of balms and drugs, of exercise where bodies learnt of things forgotten. I said to him our ancient precepts of the worths of life, discoursed our deep philosophies, propounded thus our cures for social ills. The light of doubt burned low within his eye, and his curious mind began to probe and reason with me. He bade me come to him again and yet again, and I pressed him not for action, but let him come to that decision truly as of his own will.

"Nor are you just Philosopher," he said to me. "You have uncanny knowledge."

"Almost as though my words in every case were true?"

"I cannot prove you wrong. And I do find I believe these things you say. But who else will do so?"

I waited. Perhaps the seed would grow. One man in Parliament believed in me. Others would follow.

Thankfully I built my little group. A tiny voice it was, a growing voice to point the infamy of cruel laws. To urge reforms which would lift the yoke on lowly men. A voice of Truth rising up to curb the ruthless merchant, to educate the minds of all, to frown on barriers of caste and creed. One tiny point to win, and then another. To know the whisper moving through the air—this stranger man, this man not of this time, this creature from the darkness with a queer depth of mind. To see the curious look at me, and every stranger stop with narrowed eye to pass the time of day, and probe for odd stray words of thought with which to add to stories. So pleased I was, so young despite my age.

One day a hand fell on my shoulder, and day disappeared behind the prison door.

"What is this thing?" I cried to them. They mumbled talk of Treason, Witchcraft and Conspiracy. They talked of Trial, and Death. News filtered through about my friends; they had been taken too. I waited patiently to tell the Judge of this. I polished speeches to acquaint the courts with this iniquity. I sought my enemies in mind and worked at laws to so confound them.

But days walked into weeks, and trotted by the Calendar in months. No hint of trial came to me, and surly jailers shrugged from my entreaty. The year turned slowly round and so began again. The mossy walls of prison lost their strangeness, and that daily dish of gruel became the sun of day, to which the shut prisoner stretched forth his dreary soul.

The second weary year stretched wanly on. How could my purpose be fulfilled in this gray hole? The wise men of my far-off world had not conceived a place where wisdom withered, where kindness was a gallstone, where Governing was done with Club for one, Purse of Gold for other.

There was no elation in my soul when I at last elected to walk away from that place. I had my jailer lift the lantern and look into mine eye, and with the gathering of all my soul commanded him. Trance-like he fitted key into the lock, and watched with dulled comprehension as I walked the stairway free ... much as I walked that other stairway in time past.

My friends were dead, I sorrowed for them deeply, in despair. I left that place and took a name unknown, and sought a country place to live and think. What could man do, against a system so profound?

I hungered for that other time, when reason pirouetted in the sun. I cried sad tears against this savage time. I even fitted knife against my breast and sought to end the bitter gall of failure.

So gradually my spirit calmed within, and quiet thoughts and gentle aims took arms against my sea of troubles.

Some bargain I at last do make with this new land and life.

There is much here that do so please—when hoarfrost bind the land in straitened ice, or when the golden days bestir the fields to sing, and strew the ground with tumbling leaf. Methinks my waking quill might write from these old books I find, and of these tales an essence take to color and to build, and perhaps to make immortal.

If Government and Kings want not of my experience, then perchance my fate obtains to look mine eyes around and serve the picture up for coming men?

E'en now my labored words are dashed upon the hushed agog from practiced throats, and gowned and sworded players parody the bloody wheel of life at my behest, and strut upon the ever widening stage.

Perhaps thus I move me into other times, a name and fame transposed. No hint I tell of that dark womb from whence I came, lest frightened eyes withdraw, and madness be the cap to settle on my name. This cunning the narrow-eyed mentality of present men has surely taught me. If thus I deeply labor, fixed tight upon this goal, I do perceive far down the dusty lane of time a quiet fog of people treading near my grave in homage.

Then will my dust contented lie hard by my cottage where the sweet water ripples.

I remember my very first morning in Melbourne, waking up in a tent on the outskirts of the city, feeling frostbitten even though I was wearing all the clothes I owned in the world: three t-shirts; three corduroy shirts; togs; corduroy pants; jeans; a tracksuit; three jumpers; three pairs of socks; shoes; and a suit.

I remember the first night at Booth Lodge, the excitement in the air, walking through the darkness in a stupor, meeting strange people, chatting over coffee late into the night, lying awake in bed, waiting expectantly for the next day to dawn . . . and wondering what would happen.

I remember meeting teachers, radiologists, librarians, computer programmers, postmen, journalists, and other strange people who had come from far and wide, not only to join the Workshop, but to talk about their jobs, and lifestyles, and food; their ambitions, Donald Duck comics . . . and occasionally science fiction.

I remember late nights hunched over my typewriter, scoffing at the idea of writing a good short story in three or four hours, then being told to do so . . . and somehow going away and writing it in two hours.

I remember the pressure of writing those stories, working harder than I had ever worked before in my life, and feeling the exhilaration that comes only from pushing yourself to the limit of your ability.

I remember nervously handing out copies of my stories, expecting to have them verbally torn to shreds, and having them torn to shreds, and feeling better for it.

But mostly I remember us all sitting around in The Room, with Ursula cross-legged on the carpet, smoking her pipe, and laughing at stories about petrified trees, tentacled lovers, angry food, spacesuits filled with excrement, loveable dwarves, subjunctive tensions* . . . and those interminable tales about grongs. From all this was formed a brotherly bond that endured and developed among all those who lived and shared that strange world, high up in the mountains at Booth Lodge.

JOHN EDWARD CLARK

*Subjunctive Tension: a term coined by Samuel R. Delany for expressions like "He threw his head back," "He was absorbed by the surroundings," "He strained his eyes through the viewscreen," "His eyes fell on the table." In science fiction these things could happen literally!

SINGLE CHANGES

Much good science fiction follows H.G. Wells's principle: "I make one major change from the everyday world," and our first exercise was to write a piece with such a change. It is surprising what chaos one little change can bring!

We were not to state directly what change had occurred; rather, the reader was asked to guess the change from the consequences detailed in the stories. The three examples that follow contain that magical quality, the sense of wonder, which the best science fiction offers. I recommend to any reader to try to write one: you will find not only the difficulties but also the extraordinary feeling of having your mind stretched.

The basic change implicit in each story is noted after Barbara Coleman's if you wish to check your own guesses.

ROB GERRAND

David Grigg

It is nine long years now since my brother, Jon, left in the marvelous machine he made that he calls, an automobile, and there has been no word. He left, so he said, to seek other villages in the country, other towns inhabited by men such as ourselves. A dreamer, my brother Jon.

Jon was always hurrying. Vain it was for us to tell him that speed was an evil thing, a thing which could destroy men. He paid no heed. He ran everywhere, and thought and thought on inventions to carry him about faster, regardless of the consequences.

I remember watching him run. Run! And seeing his moving form moving in a slow, slow dance, as though he were not running at all, as he moved away. And when he would come back to me, seeing his movements like one affected by a fever in the limbs, all too rapid and manic.

And then he made his automobile, his device for going as fast as possible. Blasphemy it seemed, and a work of the devil. And lo, when he drove this machine, did not we see the strange shiftings of colors that came as it went, fast, oh too fast. Deepest red, or brightest blue, the colors on Jon's face as he went to and fro in his devil's chariot.

And then his mad notion of traveling to the nearest town! We are on a rise, here, and out from us, with a spy-glass, one can see indeed what seems to be other towns. But the elders have calculated the distance to the nearest of these apparitions, and find it to be near one hundred miles away: a distance never to be traveled! In the past some of the foolish set out to walk that great distance, but were never heard of again. One such, I remember, took with him flags, with which to signal back to us here. And a strange thing it was that happened to this one as we watched him with spyglasses. At first, he would signal us, and wait for our reply. But as he walked further away, we saw him signal, and we would immediately return our own message, but in our glass, we saw him stand and wait, as though he had not seen our signal, and eventually depart, without continuing the exchange.

And then my brother Jon! He left, as I have said, these many years ago, and naught have we heard of him since...

But wait, what is this? On the lane that leads through our town, still yet far away, a blazing violet blur! My spyglass out, I see in painful violet light an image of my departed brother Jon in his demon machine, fast approaching, quickly, very quickly...

The machine stops. And out steps my brother! My brother Jon! My twin brother! And yet... he has not aged at all, still as youthful, near as the day he left. And not understanding my own age. What then, Jon, have you not been gone these nine years? What, but half a year you say? Lo! The demons have taken thee! Nine years have I waited!

Pip Maddern

McKell had been out along the seashore, filming the day. He was going to enter the film in the Arts Festival in February. It had taken him exactly a year to prepare, because he wanted shots of one day from each season. The autumn and winter and spring sequences were already prepared. He had a sneaking liking for the winter one, which was sloe and dark-toned, with a faint evanescent warmth showing spread out along the tree-tops at midday. But he was prouder of the autumn and spring sequences. He had filmed an autumn fog from midnight to midday, as it gathered into its valley, settled itself for the dawn, and then stirred and rose in great thinning columns into the warmth of the upper air. The spring one had a rainstorm against sunshine in it, and much subtle and delicately-toned interplay of winds and clouds and warming earth. And now he had finished the summer shots; the gradual morning to afternoon transition of the balance of heat from the sea to the beach, until the brilliant stripe of dry sand almost hurt one's eyes.

On the way home, he stepped on a snake. It must have been lying quite motionless on the path, so all he ever saw of it was a snake-shaped piece of ground flowing into the undergrowth after it had struck his ankle.

He knew his snake-bite drill, but his hands were shaking so that he could hardly adjust the tourniquet. There was a knife in his kit, too, but he couldn't feel the punctures in his leg, and didn't think that indiscriminate slashing would help. After that, there was nothing for him to do but keep moving—as calmly and carefully as possible. He calculated he was at least four miles from the nearest town, where he was staying. And then again, the snake might not have been a poisonous one.

He kept hoping that until his leg began to swell, and throb, and drag at the ground. By that time, his head was aching badly. He still kept walking, hoping to meet someone on the path. But he had deliberately chosen an out-of-the-way beach to work on, and when he looked down the cooling alley between the trees, there was no one coming.

His leg hurt, so he sat down to rest. When he tried to get up again, he couldn't. He crawled a little farther, but it made him very tired, and he was more than reasonably afraid of setting his hand on another snake.

He sat down again, with his back to a tree. It occurred to him that if no one came, he would die, and by morning his body would have faded out of sight. He wished very much that snakes were visible.

Barbara J. Coleman

Margaret Colway felt a generation older the day her first husband died. She had never thought that it would affect her the way it did, but then, she had never really known just how she would feel when the inevitable came.

Many times she had seen men die; men curled up in pain and their wives beside them, weeping. She had thought she would grow accustomed to it, but now she felt depressed and very lonely.

As soon as she reached her room after returning from the Urology ward, she rang her mother and asked her to come and talk, over lunch. At twelve o'clock Margaret rang her assistant down in Pathology.

"Hello, Kate? If anyone wants me before two, I'm going out. I'll have my pager with me, but I'd prefer it if it wasn't used—you understand, don't you?"

"Certainly, Doctor," replied Kate sympathetically, "and I was very sorry to hear about David this morning..."

"Thank you. Actually, I'm having lunch with mother. I'll see you later."

Doreen Colway was a statuesque woman in her midfifties, with gray hair neatly brushed into a bun and no attempt to disguise the lines around her eyes and mouth. She was wise in the ways of life, and death. While she waited in the bistro for her daughter, she contemplated the years behind her.

She remembered how she had felt when her first husband had died. Ah yes—dear Neville; they had only been married four months. Then there had been Richard, Franco and Lou, Margaret's father.

None had been married for more than two years before they had died. There had been others since, four to be exact. It was strange now, that the first husband of her youngest daughter was gone; it was a milestone, almost as much as the birth of a grandchild. It almost made her feel like a venerable matriarch...she smiled at the thought.

Margaret came in and sat down heavily. Her mother looked at her gently.

"My poor, dear girl! It *has* shaken you, hasn't it?"

"Yes. I...I feel so much *older,* and I really miss him."

"There's always a first time; I had it, we all have it."

"I know. That's the hellish bit. And I've seen it from every angle—now."

"Well, there's only one thing worse than losing a husband, my dear, especially a first or a particularly beloved one. That's the first *son.*"

"Oh, I'm *dreading* it. Micky's nearly two now, and I really wish he wouldn't grow up and into danger. I mean, from their thirteenth birthday onwards you start worrying about their health. And when the end comes, it comes so suddenly, so horribly."

"Yes, indeed it does. And a son is not like a husband at all. It gets easier to attract a male as you get older, but come the change of life, and there are no more children at all... And when all the boys are gone—well, that's it, isn't it?"

"As you say. And because it comes so unexpectedly for any man you can't let them go too far away, unless they're married, or study too much because they won't live long enough to use what they've learned..."

"Well, there *are* more men taking courses such as Engineering, Accountancy and Secretarial practice these days, you know. David was one—and in his last year at Tech school..."

"Progress in research is going so slowly though..." mused her daughter.

"And," said Doreen curiously, as she broke her bread into the soup, "just what is *new* there?"

"I was talking to Hilda Brown the other day, and she thinks that there is some hormone link. Also, it might soon be possible to detect it with a hormone test, rather like the usual pregnancy test for women.

Earlier, we hope, than we now detect them—which is when they develop pain, serious internal ruptures and urinary blockage. That's what kills them so quickly."

"Really?" said Doreen. "How would it be treated?"

"By a rather radical operation. Of course, you'd have to remove most of the prostate, ova, and everything in between. It would damage their urinary system and leave them sterile for life—a rather serious thing for a boy in his teens or twenties."

"Gracious me! Sounds very gory. I suppose then you'd be running into ethical considerations. They wouldn't be able to be married, and after all, what use is a sterile male?"

"Yes," Margaret considered. "There are all sorts of social attitudes that will probably have to change. After all, with this problem solved it's quite possible that men might even be able to live into their forties..."

She nibbled at her salad as she talked, gradually feeling so much better for being able to talk over her emotions and thoughts on the matter; it was eventually a quarter to three before she returned to the hospital.

James Finch, a strapping young lad with blonde hair and blue eyes, had just brought coffee into her room when she arrived. Today he hoped that he would make some impression on her; he'd trimmed his beard and hair and was extremely pleasant and efficient. He had also heard about David. Jim liked Dr. Colway. She was a very pleasant, mature woman, the sort of woman that a man really needed.

Margaret smiled at him as he left. She was a little shocked at herself for thinking about another husband before David had been buried! Then she remembered that she ought to ring David's mother.

The Single Changes

The preceding examples were read aloud to an audience at the 33rd World Science Fiction Convention, and people were asked to see if they could work out what the changes were. David's story was called "The Tyranny of Distance" and is based on the fascinating idea of a world where the speed of light is only ten miles per hour. Pip Maddern's was called "Infra Red," and that gives the game away. Barbara Coleman's was called "The First Time Hurts the Most" and deals with a biological change: a hormone problem in the human male that causes them to become parthenogenetically pregnant in their vestigial "womb" beneath the prostate gland. The main consequence of this is that the "ectopic" pregnancy quickly ruptures fatally; a danger to any male over puberty.

THE LOVE STORIES

The Love Story was our greatest challenge. It sent us searching into our deepest levels. What was love, anyway? A cliché, if it existed at all? The most moving experience we had undergone? A device for seducing the sex opposite? Whatever we felt the answer might be, it led us immediately to the questions: who experiences it? And how do we convey it?

The Love Stories were probably the strongest stories we produced; the false, the gimmicky, the faking stood out and could not be so easily got away with.

ROB GERRAND

David Grigg

Introduction

The dormitories where we slept were two-storied, and the ground floor as well as containing bedrooms had a large living area with a small kitchen and a huge table and lots of chairs. This evening, as for many nights before, the living room was full of people trying to grind out ideas so they could set to work on their assignments. Working like this proved to many of us that you really don't need peace and quiet to compose: all you need is not to be directly interrupted.

Andrew Whitmore sat at the table tapping out another word every so often on his typewriter, and then sitting back with his eyes glazed.

The fact was that Andrew had not slept at all the previous night, as he had stayed awake completing a story written entirely without adjectives or adverbs. His condition now, approaching midnight, was not that of a sane man. I envied his stamina, but not his single-mindedness.

Over in the kitchen area, Derrick Ashby was waiting for the electric jug to boil so that he could prepare another round of black coffee for everyone.

But me, I had still to set typewriter to paper. As yet, I hadn't had a single idea. How does one begin to write a love story? A science-fiction love story, at that. Various images of humans making love to aliens, to robots, or vice-versa, had passed through my head and been discarded. I was becoming desperate. How could I show my face tomorrow if I didn't have a story to submit? "A *love* story!" I muttered again.

I was pacing backwards and forwards, which was not entirely

easy, for as well as the people sitting around the table in front of their mute typewriters, the floor was littered with screwed-up paper, and there were even a few people lying there attempting, it seemed, to drum up ideas by simulating sleep. Annis Shepherd sat beneath the stairs, chewing the end of her pencil. Annis lived in the other dormitory, but she had come round because she said that the atmosphere was better here. At least, nobody smoked. But her presence was not encouraging, for she kept on saying: "I can't *do* it!"

Derrick brought the black coffee to the table, moved aside the typewriters and piles of rejected paper, and put the cups down. Everyone reached quickly for this source of stimulation. Andrew in particular grasped at the coffee like a man on his deathbed reaching for the elixir of life.

"A love story! It's impossible! I'll never do it!" I said. Robert Young looked up from his manuscript. "You always go on like this," he said, "and yet you always seem to think of something."

Knowing that didn't help me while I was pacing. And this time I didn't even have a starting piont.

From a nearby bedroom I heard a sudden shout of triumph, and a typewriter began clattering at high speed. Bruce Gillespie, I thought, you bastard! Upstairs, the few lucky people who had already finished their stories and photocopied them were blissfully asleep.

All through the room people sat looking blankly at equally blank sheets of paper in typewriters, or gazing into the air, or chewing their fingernails. Perhaps little was as yet being written, but several minds were imagining great plots and strange characters. Not mine, though.

Andrew began typing again, a little faster than before. Either the black coffee had done him some good or the sound of rapid typing coming from Bruce's room had prodded him.

The photocopier was located in Dormitory One. It sat by the door and gave off the kind of fumes that photocopiers do. Living in the same dormitory as the photocopier was convenient when I wanted to run off a story, but it also meant that I had several times been awakened at very strange hours while some exhausted soul ran off his story before collapsing.

The door to the outside world opened, letting in a blast of cold mountain air, and Bruce Barnes from the other dormitory, brandishing a manuscript. "Finished!" he cried, gloating. Everyone in the room glared at him as he proceeded to run off twenty copies of his story.

I had stopped looking at the clock. It was a reminder that I had still not begun to work on the assignment, and that there were only a diminishing number of hours before I had to be up for breakfast and into the workshop session again. The assignments would not be discussed until the afternoon, but it was considered the done thing not to miss out on the morning's work to finish an assignment. That didn't stop people putting the finishing touches to their work during lunch; but if you were to wait until then you were clearly having real trouble.

But it was no good. I still didn't have an idea. Finally, in despair, I picked up Roget's Thesaurus. "Derrick," I said, "give me a number between one and one thousand."

"Three hundred and forty-nine," he said without hesitation, and went back to typing.

I flipped rapidly through the book, looking for entry 349. I found it: "ISLAND."

Island . . . islands . . . "No man is an island entire of itself" . . . I began pacing the floor again, and a story slowly began to take shape in my head, and with it, a strange joy. It was a joy I'd known before, when I had finally put my two random words together and made an image of them.

I found a spot at the table, and pulled a typewriter toward me. It happened to be the machine I had brought to the workshop. Typewriters seemed to swap backwards and forwards all through the workshop, so that it was rare that you were using your own machine. I picked up a piece of paper, inserted it in the machine, and typed:

ISLANDS, by David Grigg.

Several crumpled sheets of paper later, I had worked out how to begin. If there was one thing I had learned at the workshop, it was that the first three pages of my first attempt at a story could be discarded as irrelevant. Once I had thrown those three pages away, I was ready to begin the real story.

All around me, people were rattling away at their typewriters or, like Andrew, pecking out a word every few minutes. Under the stairs, Annis was scribbling furiously. There was a final cry of triumph from Bruce Gillespie's room, and I heard the sound of a piece of paper being pulled from a typewriter, then the sound of a body falling heavily onto a bed. Robert Young despaired of his story and went to make some more black coffee.

At some stage I knew exactly how it would end, and I seemed to be slowed down only by the limited speed at which I could type. Time passed. At one point I looked up and there was only Andrew and Derrick and myself left in the room, all hammering at typewriters with harrowed expressions on our faces. And there seemed then, among the three of us, if I did not imagine it, a genuine feeling of comradeship, of mutual striving. It was very encouraging.

Still later, I finished the first draft of my story, and looked up in exhaustion. Only Andrew was left on the other side of the table, still pecking away.

I should have gone to bed. It was a quarter past two in the morning. I had to be up at eight. But I wanted to redraft the story, and type it out without the many mistakes and crossouts so that it would be readable once photocopied.

So I stood up and moved to the electric typewriter that Andrew had brought with him but never used himself. I turned it on and started typing again. It was easier on my sore fingers.

At last I tore the final page from the machine and stumbled to the copier. It was three A.M. The copying finished, I grabbed a stapler and collated the pages. I was beginning to hate that story. It seemed to be on my back, around my throat, forcing me to keep moving when I wanted to drop. Then it was all done, and I picked myself up and staggered toward my bedroom.

But before I closed the door, I turned back to Andrew, who was, incredibly, still typing. The expression on his face was that of a man possessed.

"Goodnight, Andrew," I said.

"Mumble," said Andrew, and tapped out another word.

David Grigg

Islands

They came together high above the ecliptic, twin moving stars in an empty universe.

As soon as Mikhail saw the other asteroid—a tiny flickering point amongst the constellations—he went in through the airlock and turned on the communicator, hoping to pick up the sound of another human voice. It had been a long time.

So when her voice came crackling out of the speaker, and the first static-filled image swam onto the screen, his feelings were of great joy.

They were still light-minutes distant, of course, and would be so for some time yet, but Mikhail began speaking as soon as he picked up the other's signal.

"Hello," he said, "I'm Mikhail Brinski. My asteroid's Elaine. Who's there?" Then he sat back and waited. Feelings that had been dormant within him through a long winter had stirred at the first sound of a human voice.

"Janys here. My rock's the Isolde. Who's out there? Are you a miner? That's what I am, after tin."

Mikhail pushed himself away from the console, and stared at the distorted image on the screen. His own words, he knew, had not reached her yet. "Janys?" he said, for his own ears, not for hers. *Janys?*

Was it possible? Out here? An old, old pain throbbed again within him: Janys? *That* Janys?

Her voice came again, startled, urgent: "Mikhail Brinski? From Vostok? Do I know you from Vostok? Vostok and London?"

"Yes," he said, again to himself. "Yes, from Vostok." He almost turned off the screen and speaker. *That* Janys. It was. And of everything, it was the anger he remembered, the hurt from those days.

Vostok and London. It had been London where she'd left him. London where they had met, Vostok where they had loved. And London again. London in the quiet green park, and her walking away along an endless sun-striped lane of trees. London.

At last, he said out loud to the wavering face on the screen: "Yes, Janys, it's the Mikhail you knew." He forced a smile to his face. "How long is it now? And what are you doing chasing rocks up here? Weren't there enough on Earth for you?" He could not keep the sadness out of his voice. Perhaps it wouldn't show. Perhaps she might ignore it. She had been good at that sort of thing, had Janys.

To keep his mind still, he looked at the instrument readings and forced his mind to absorb what they said. The faltering pinprick of light indicating the other asteroid still trembled in the center of the viewscreen.

Mikhail hung in the center of a floating chaos. Since moving out into the Belt, he had become a sloppy hermit. His untidiness on Earth had always been a failing; out here it was worse. Broken pencils, papers, microfilms, cannisters of food and all the other kinds of kipple that made up Mikhail's monastic life wandered like a miniature asteroid swarm of their own around his room. Now Mikhail himself drifted there, feeling very lost, very much alone, watching the woman on the screen.

The image was slowly improving: the two planetoids were getting closer in their orbits. The time lag would get shorter, too.

"Hello, Mikhail," came her voice. There was an expression on her face that he found hard to interpret. Was it pity? "It's been six years, I think. I've been working hard. What am I doing up here? What are *you* doing? I thought you were going to go back to Moscow to work on your maths? Well, you know, I got sick of trying to sniff out new ores on Earth. There weren't any!"

"Do you remember . . ." he said before he could stop himself. For a brief instant, he wished he could chase after his words and fetch them back. Do you remember . . . how it was?

It had been in London's dirty winter. The pure snow that had fallen days before had become the filthy slush that now lay in the streets. They'd met at the Technic, shared a few classes, though their majors were different, and he had started walking her home to her flat in one of the dingy, endless terraces that still existed then. And that day, walking with soaked boots through the slush, she'd suddenly stopped and looked up at him.

"I like you, you mathematical mastermind," she'd said, "I do. Come up to my room." And he, startled into new emotions, had gone up.

"Yes," said Janys, from the clearing screen, "Yes, I remember, Mikhail. It is a long time, but I do. Yes." She smiled and looked away from the camera for a moment, away from his eyes. "How do you find it up here? Gets lonely, a bit. But the view's the best for miles. When I first went mining, I became a regular tourist. You know, kept taking photos of all the stars, pictures of my very own asteroid at a distance, and all that. Then I realized I was crazy: if I stayed where I was I wouldn't need to remind myself with pictures, would I?"

He smiled a polite smile for her. "No," he said, "no, you wouldn't." The time delay was down to about twenty seconds, now. It would get less. "As for why I'm here . . . Well, I'm still working on my maths. It needs a lot of quiet, a lot of thought. I'm being a bit of a hermit, living in a kind of ivory tower to end all ivory towers." The picture of her face was clearer: he could see new lines. But he could still not see through her face to see what she thought.

He wished for an instant he could go outside and just watch the asteroid that she had called Elaine getting closer, to use his eyes directly, to remove the barriers, somehow. In the viewscreen at least, the rock was now a tiny slowly turning pebble.

They had gone fossicking up in the hills in the spring, she looking for samples of rock, and he just for the peace, to think. She'd captured a photo of him sitting just like the statue of Rodin, chin in hand, and shown it to all their friends. At the top of a crag, he'd pulled up a flower and solemnly proffered it to her. She'd made him replant it, scolding him all the way.

It was strange. They had first talked of spacing one day on the moors amongst all the harsh glory of the Earth. Somehow the thought of space had seemed more glamorous then, more romantic.

The scenes that the Brontës had described seemed of another age, past, forgotten. So, sitting on the heather, they had talked of the planets, the new expeditions out past Mars. He had been the more interested, and she had teased him about his fascination: "Two plus two is four wherever you are, isn't it? Or will we have to learn our sums again on Jupiter?"

"Maths is the same," he'd said, "but people aren't."

Isolde and Elaine, rocky sisters, were at opposition. The time delay on the radio was as short as it would be: five seconds.

"I'm doing some work on the Kroeger functions," he said, seeking any trace of old affection in her face on the screen. "In another six months, I should have a paper for the Journal. I'm getting quite well known..."

"Well known to all your stuffy professors, Mikhail, but I'll bet there's hardly a Belter knows you're out here. But I'm glad for you. Did I tell you I'm thinking of leaving the System?"

"The solar system?"

"I've applied to go out on the *Transstar:* they'll need good geologists." Her smile now was more honest, more open.

Mikhail stirred amongst his floating rubbish, realizing for the first time she could see his littered surroundings. What he could see of the cabin she was in was very neat, everything clipped into place. He felt drained: his hands had at last stopped trembling; they seemed to have absorbed a kind of numbness.

"How have you been, Janys?" he said.

"Pretty well," she said. "Jason went out to Callisto, did you know? I was...well, pretty lonely after that, but, well, it's gone."

"Being on your own in space is rather strange," he said, "but somehow it seems, I don't know, more acceptable out here..." He looked around him for a second, looking at the slowly shifting debris, looked back with a small, embarrassed laugh: "Sorry for the mess."

"You always said that! You never got neater, though. Your mother trained you very badly." There seemed a softness in her eyes, a look, perhaps, of understanding.

He smiled at her gentle scolding, and shrugged.

Summer had been in Vostok: Mikhail's home town. With the

new government, everything was changing very rapidly. Everything had seemed bustling, busy, uncertain. They had lived together there for the season.

She would drag him along to the market each week to buy their vegetables and meat, against his protests. He had tagged behind her like a tall, shy puppy, threading his way through the crowds, trying to keep up. Then she would load him up with parcels, one on top of the other until he nearly dropped them, and he would smile at her over the top of his burdens.

Perhaps it was in Vostok, though, that there had come harsher notes into their mutual symphony. It could have been their closer proximity. It could have been the city. She had talked of going to Australia in search of the rarer minerals. He had wanted to go to Moscow to meet some of the mathematicians there. There had been arguments, and tears, in Vostok.

The delay was increasing again: the worldlets were drawing apart. He seemed to look as often at the diminishing asteroid as he did at Janys' face.

Mikhail tugged at his chin with his hand, drifted away a little from the screen. "It's good to see you, Janys."

There was a pause as the radio waves traversed the space between them. A little longer, perhaps. She made a small frown, scolding him a little again, and said: "It's been nice to see you, too, Mikhail. It's fun to remember old times." A brief burst of static obscured her face, and when he could see her again, the frown was gone. "You remember that time in Vostok," she said, "the day we bought that doll? You know, the kind that fit inside one another, right down to the smallest little doll? I've still got that, here in my rock." She went off the screen for a moment, returned with the doll. The picture was getting worse: Janys seemed to have a soft ghost beside her. The speaker was beginning to crackle.

"I've still got the photo you took of me as the Thinker," he said. "Somewhere in here..."

He watched her silent, attentive face for the long, long seconds to pass before she responded with a smile: fresh, even teeth.

In the end, they decided to go back to London. The trees in Hyde Park had turned to gold. They went walking there, very often. But there seemed to be something that had distanced them: they touched, and it was as if they touched only a pane of glass that stood between them.

He talked more of his work to her, she more of hers to him. She needed to travel, to dig, to pick up rocks, to test sites. His need was to be still, quiet, thinking within himself.

And at last, in late autumn, he had sat still on the park bench, watching her walk away, knowing she would not turn back.

Static patterned the screen: he could hardly glimpse her face any more. It was hard to pick up what she said. He spent long minutes waiting for her replies.

"It was good," she said, "good to talk."

"Yes," he said, "very good . . ."

The minutes passed. The picture was all static now, as the asteroids moved on in their inevitable orbits. But at last, half obscured by hiss and noise, her voice came back: "Farewell, my love . . ."

He nodded, smiled softly. "Farewell."

John Edward Clark

Emily, My Emily

Emily won't speak to me. She just sits there staring. Staring, staring, staring. Glaring. Not saying anything.

Maybe it was something I did. Maybe it was something I said. Maybe I shouldn't have called her a slut.

"I'm sorry, Emily. I didn't mean to hurt you."

I rub my red eyes.

But she still doesn't respond. Emily won't speak to me. She just sits in the back of the lifeboat staring at me.

She's been like that for three days now. And I'm worried. I'm going crazy.

"Speak to me, Emily. Speak to me, please?"

Silence.

"Whisper sweet nothings into my ear?"

Silence.

"Speak to me you slut!"

Silence.

"I'm sorry, Emily. I didn't mean that, sweetheart."

What am I doing? What am I saying? I'm going crazy!

She used to speak to me, you know. She used to whisper sweet nothings into my ear. Ah, Emily was so romantic...once. She used to smile at me and say, "I love you I love you I love you." She used to smile at me and say, "Fuck the living daylights out of me, big boy!"

Emily is like that. Her moods change a lot.

"Speak to me!" I cry. "I've got to hear your voice!"

Emily, my Emily, is my only companion in this motionless lifeboat. Emily, my Emily, is my only reason for still being alive. Emily, my Emily, is my life-size, inflatable doll.

And I just realized I'm going crazy.

I'm frightened. I grab the canteen and swallow a mouthful of water, nervously. It spills from my trembling lips.

"Get a grip on yourself," I tell myself quite firmly.

Get a grip on yourself? I've been doing little else for the past four days.

I masturbate a lot. But I can't think of anything else to do. I'm going crazy.

I have to admit, Emily's a good-looking chick. She reminds me a lot of my wife. She's got soft blue eyes, and blonde hair, and brown thighs, and smooth skin, and long slender legs, and a pretty face, and breasts the size of rock melons.

I love her.

And she won't speak to me.

And I'm going crazy.

It's been weeks now. Yeah, about five weeks since the ship came down. I think. I can still hear the screams in my ears. They're dead now, all of them. But the screams remain. I can hear them. Sometimes they're so loud I can't sleep. Sometimes they're so loud I can't think.

I remember the mad scramble for the lifeboats. People screaming, running, falling, slipping in blood. I remember the fight the old man put up when I tried to take his bag. He was a jeweler, and he carried that black bag with him everywhere. I thought it must have contained about a million dollars in diamonds, and rubies, and sapphires. It didn't. It contained Emily.

I had to kill him to get the bag. I didn't want to. He put up such a fight, biting, and scratching, and clawing, and spitting blood. He was mad. He fell and hit his head on a desktop. It was an accident. I didn't mean to kill him.

Jesus. I killed a man for a life-size inflatable doll...

But, Jesus—it was worth it!

What am I saying? I'm going crazy.

"Speak to me, Emily!"

Emily just sits there in the back of the lifeboat, saying nothing.

Her voice recorder must be broken. Maybe I could stick my hand in her throat, and fix it up? I'd be gentle, ever so gentle. It might only be a twisted tape loop, or a jammed cog, or a fluff of dust in the machinery. She won't feel a thing. I'll just reach down and...

No. I couldn't do that to Emily.

Frustrated, I turn and look out across the still sea. There's no wind. There's no sound but my own labored breathing, and the ceaseless bleep-bleep-bleep of my bleeper sending out the distress signal.

The sea is pale white and shimmering. It's one great sheet of waxed glass. It's menacing, eerie, and dead. It's like acid.

I know it's like acid because the other day I slipped my right hand into it and now I've only got three fingers left.

I've sutured and bandaged the wound, but it still hurts sometimes.

I hope they come and rescue me from this God-forsaken planet.

I hope they come and rescue me and Emily.

I love Emily. Emily is my wife.

Ah Emily, how do I love you? Let me count the ways. I love you to the length and breadth and depth of this endless ocean. I love you to . . .

What am I saying?

I'm going crazy!

She's only a doll, a bloody doll—not flesh and blood and bones. Not real, live, living. Only rubber and plastic and glue and paint. A doll.

"Speak to me, Emily!"

Emily does not reply. She just sits there in the back of the lifeboat, saying nothing.

How did we get into this mess, anyway? It was supposed to be a simple express flight. Goron to Antares. Zip! Why did the Captain have to get drunk? Why did we have to take a detour? Why did the engines have to stall? Why, why, why?

I was lucky to get out alive. There were thirty people on board ship, and I was the only one that got away. I can still hear their screams. Yes, I was lucky. The explosion nearly sank the raft. It knocked me out—I must have been carried some distance by the explosive swell. The ship's gone. There's no wreckage left. Nothing. The sea has swallowed the dead. And now it's hungry for me. I can feel it watching, waiting.

"I'm scared, Emily."

Emily is the most important thing in my life. It's the tiny, unimportant things I like most about her. The way she twirls strands of hair between her fingers when she's thinking. The way her face broods when she thinks nobody's watching. The freckles on her face. Her ear lobes. Her shiny plastic skin.

Hey? I'm going crazy. Plastic skin? That's not Emily...

I shake my head roughly, and wipe the sweat from my face. Everything will be all right. Just stay calm. Think. Hold onto your mind. Forget about her. Forget about that doll over there. Forget how randy you are. Hold onto your mind.

I drop my hand to my side, and play with the cuff of my trousers. My fingers wander. They close around something solid. I lift it up slowly, and nonchalantly examine it. It's a book. It has a plain brown cover. It's called *How to Make Love to a Life-Size Inflatable Doll.*

Jesus! I remember now, it came in the bag with Emily.

"Emily, I love you.

"What? Did you say something Emily?

"Don't tease me Emily, please don't tease me. Speak to me. Don't be cruel."

Oh my God my God my God. She's hissing at me.

Oh my God my God my God. She's sprung a leak!

I try to fix her up with a bandage, but it's no good. It won't hold.

I'm sorry Emily. I don't have any patches, or glue—not even a bandaid. I tried Emily, I really did. If only I had a bandaid. I can't bear to look at her anymore. Emily, my Emily. Just sits there in the back of the lifeboat, staring down. She looks old and very, very tired. She's crumpled, and shrunken, and wrinkled, and shriveled. She just sits there in a heap. And she won't speak to me.

I hide my face in my wet hands, and cry. Emily, Emily, Emily. I whimper. I'm a very emotional person.

"Hello!"

What? Did you say something, Emily?

"Hello there!"

She did. She did say something. She's still alive! Emily is still alive!

I wipe my eyes and look up at her.

But Emily hasn't moved. She's still lying there in a listless heap at the back of the lifeboat. She won't move. She won't talk. She can't move. She can't talk. She's only a bundle of plastic. I suddenly realize the truth. That's only a life-size inflatable doll with a hole in its side, over there. That's not my Emily. Emily is a million miles away—safe on Antares.

"Hello down there! Are you okay?"

A gust of warm wind moves my hair. I look up into the burning sky. There's a gray spaceship hovering overhead, firing blasts of air down from its retro rockets, sending rough ripples out across the sea, rocking my tiny lifeboat like a cork.

I'm saved! Saved!

Reality comes flooding back into my mind. I'm not crazy anymore. I know what I am, who I am, where I am. I'm Roger Valdom. I'm a galactic insurance salesman, and a part-time thief. I'm alone on a lifeboat in the middle of a sea of acid with a shoddy life-size inflatable doll that I stole from a little old man after I killed him.

I'm not crazy at all.

They'll be picking me up soon. I'll be going home—back to Antares. Back to Emily. I'll wrap my arms around her, and hug her, and cuddle her waist, and slip my fingers through her shining hair, and kiss the freckles on her face, and tickle her earlobes, and tell her I love her.

"I love you, Emily, I love you."

And I'm not crazy anymore.

I can see them standing on the observation deck, looking down at me. They're coming to get me. They'll be picking me up soon. They'll be taking me home.

"I love you, Emily, I love you."

Sniffling back tears, I look up at the sky and wave my arms wildly.

"I love you, Emily, I love you."

I cry.

I hope someone on board's got a bandaid.

Rob Gerrand

Song and Dance

Jenny walked along the path, high on the side of the valley.

The earth was hard, well-trodden. It wound around occasional outcroppings of rock. Grass and wildflowers grew to both sides, the hill rose high up to her right. Way down below was the river from which her tribe took sustenance.

She raised her head, carefully surveying the sky. There was no sign of cloud. Clear blue it was, clear blue it would remain.

What am I? she thought. I feel my body. It is me, it is working. She folded both hands, watching her fists form. It was good to be alive.

She turned her mind away from the lessons of obloquy and cant, ratiocination and pansogmatism.

Instead she was aware of a breeze at her neck, the sun on her bare arms and legs. The sun!

She loved to come up amongst the high hills, away from details, the dullness of the village. Here she felt free, here she could lie down, roll in the grass, hug the earth. Here she could gaze up, let her mind soar. Here she could look the long drop down, and if she chose, here she could descend either quickly or slowly.

She sat down then, placed her hands behind her back and stared up into the sky, letting the blue invade softly her head, her mind opening and eyes closing, her shoulders gradually slipping to the ground. She moved her right arm over her forehead.

Her body relaxed, a warm soothing spreading throughout her body. She slept.

111

She sensed a shadow, and opened her eyes. A figure standing over her—startled, she thought:

Who are you?

Such strange garments, red and yellow, smiling eyes, staring, amused.

"Hello."

How strange. As Jenny caught his greeting a melodious sound disturbed her ears. His mouth had moved, oh subtly.

Who are you? I am Jenny.

"My name? People call me Madness, they call me many names."

Again that disturbing song intruded, but a lilting rippling babble, it was. Oh, how describe it? It would need such a big-throated bird to sound such low rich notes.

What magic-mind was this, creating sounds upon the air, such embroidered illustrations of his thoughts?

"Call me Madness, or Evil, or Sickness."

But where do you come from? Why are you here?

"It is fine blue afternoon, the sun still in the sky."

You don't look sick, or evil.

He bowed. "Other names some are kind enough to bestow. What it means I do not know."

She saw his face, clear and generous.

I like you.

"You are curious, Jenny. I like your bright eyes. And here you lie alone, on the high hillside."

My people work down there. I wander. I wonder. I ponder.

"I must dance for you." And gracefully he turned, and stepped and swung, a strange humming tune like no bird song accompanying his dance.

"Come Jenny, dance." He reached in a fluid movement, her hand was grasped, she was on her feet, and flying with his arms. Sky flashed, toes skipped, arms linked, sun winked.

"Ah," he sang, "philosophers have their theories, their theories. We have our sweet memories.

"Do you not feel as I feel?"

It was true, this fierce urge to merge. She was entranced, their flying bodies whistling in the air. So happily he entertained her, what sparkling bubbling brooks he sounded for her ears.

A breathless pause. He held her, closely looking in her eyes.

"Ah Jenny, do you feel? I fear you don't. You're not with me." He stepped back, head drooped, turned to leave.

In Jenny something deep closed up in dismay. Why did he leave? How could she keep this flighty magic boy?

Don't go, she thought. Still sing, still dance. Please stay.

Her thoughts returned his gaze, he searched her face. He smiled, he sighed relief. Delight was in his eyes.

But what had she to offer? Simple village girl, no songs, no sounds could she make. Was he—?

He was making mockery.

"No. No." Two deep tones reinforced his protestations. He danced reassurance, while speaking of her beauty.

Timidly she listened, bashfully she let him introduce her to the dance once more. Until they rolled united on the ground.

"The sun sets soon," a whispery sound caressed her cheeks. He was gone, dancing up the path. "Tomorrow," she heard his call.

Next afternoon he was waiting for her when she arrived.

"I thought you might not come," he said.

The sounds that greeted her seemed harsh, without the life of yesterday.

She looked at him, puzzled.

You cannot hear my thoughts?

"No. I cannot. I have a new dance for you." He stepped back, raised his arms, started to sing and sway.

Jenny watched his feet dance on the hard brown earth she knew. She looked at the grass, and sat to feel it, looked up at her sky, clear blue again.

The sounds ceased. She turned her head.

"You don't wish to dance?"

I am looking at the blue.

"I will look at the blue too."

Jenny lay back. But it was difficult to relax with her noisy companion. She looked down at her tiny distant village.

I think I shall go home.

"But you have hardly come. We haven't talked, or anything."

I walk each afternoon.

Each day she found him waiting, and she was amused from time to time. She allowed him to make love. But it seemed to Jenny that her walks no longer held the treasured peace. She came less often, and walked instead along the river. Each time she saw him, the silly singing seemed so insistent, distracting, she asked him not to come.

My path is different now—it is disturbed.

But when she climbed the high hills still she found him, driven to wilder dances, more raucous singing.

Leave me my peace, she thought in anger. Have you not understood?

But louder he sang, more furiously he danced, feet flying, a febrile blur.

Leave me! You are obsessed, your noise distresses me. Oh, you are mad.

Still on he danced, a broken sobbing rasping in his voice. He would not stop.

Jenny moved nearer the flying limbs, and gave a swift nudge.

He fell, fell into the valley toward the river, became a speck, which swooped and rose the other side, up, up and disappeared over the mountains.

Bruce Gillespie

Vegetable Love

"Welcome to the cave of signs," said the tourist guide. She held the microphone lightly in her hand, pointed the shoulder speaker toward us, and stared out of the window of the tourist bubble. "When you alight from the craft, you are advised to wear your protective clothing at all times. The walls of the cave sometimes emit irritating gases."

The interior of the cave did not look at all dangerous as we stepped out of the tourist bubble onto its spongy floor. Waves of green light flowed over us from the roof. The floor itself looked like the slope of a well-kept park. In the light gravity, we bounced, rather than walked, toward the far wall of the cave. Petals and ferns sprouted briefly in front of our footsteps, but just as often they sank back into the floor or deflected their stems courteously as we passed by.

"The chief aesthetic interest of the cave of signs," the tourist guide went on to inform us, while making a creditable attempt to speak and walk at the same time, "is its apparent ability to listen sympathetically to people who speak to it. It appears to speak back to us by means of changing gradations in the rich pigments within its walls. Scientists believe that the living tissue of this cave is the galaxy's only known entity to welcome communication with human beings."

"I don't believe that," said the elderly lady loping along beside me, trying to keep up with the rest of the tourist party. "When he was alive, my husband believed firmly that human beings should never talk to aliens."

115

"Nobody knows whether the cave speaks back to us or not," I said, trying not to evade conversation too obviously. "Maybe the cave just performs cheap party tricks for the stupid Earthmen so we will go away and leave it alone."

I rather wished that I could get away myself. I had only one reason for being here. I cared little for this expedition or the other people in the tourist party. My answer stopped the old lady from continuing the conversation, and I could now concentrate on the important business at hand.

She had been wearing her tourist-guide's uniform when I saw her that first time in the cafe at the spaceport. She had been sitting at a table, talking to another guide, drinking coffee, and I had sat beside her, because there were no other empty seats in the cafe. I looked up after examining the menu; she looked up from her coffee; I asked her out for dinner.

She talked little during dinner and gave me no encouragement. The more that expression of disdain settled over her face, the more beautiful she looked to me. At the door of the hotel, she slipped neatly from under my arm and closed the door behind her quickly and firmly. When I rang the hotel desk the next morning, I discovered that, unexpectedly she had been called to conduct the tourist trip to Lucya from Earth. She looked annoyed when she saw that I had managed to board the craft at the last moment and was a passenger on her flight. She solved the problem of my presence by ignoring it altogether. Each hour that passed, the more convinced I became that I would follow her to the end of the universe, if need be. Which is more or less what I did.

I found that I had run ahead of the rest of the tourist party and had caught up with our guide. Surely she would talk to me now that I had her alone? "I've heard that the cave makes a display of pretty lights if it likes you," I said, trying to make conversation. I blushed when I realized that I was merely repeating words from her own spiel.

"Really, Mr. Trella," she said, somehow remaining cool and distant while striding ahead like an athlete. "Surely you have read Rafael Reich's famous book about the cave of signs? Even Reich, who has specialized in studying this cave, cannot explain, for instance, the amazing correspondences between aspirations verbalized by visitors to the cave, and the changes which take place in people's lives after they leave here."

"You mean that it's like a huge wishing well?" I said. I was so surprised that I nearly missed the cue. It was the first time that she had responded to any remark of mine since our meeting in the cafe and the frosty dinner afterward.

"It's not just like a blarney stone, if that's what you mean," she said. An eager expression showed in her face. She was beginning to warm to her subject, if not to me. "Reich actually performed specific experiments here. He would place a key or a watch on a rock in one part of the cave. He would wish it to reappear in another part of the cave, and occasionally it would. Usually this happened only when the cave was making its display of colors.

"You know, Mr. Trella"—she looked directly into my face for the first time—"once I made a wish in here to find a precious locket I had lost. The next day, I found it squeezed into the lining of my bag. This place works."

I was just about to ask whether the cave of signs conjured up the affections of attractive tourist guides when we reached our destination, the wall most distant from the tourist bubble. The rest of the group caught up with us, and crowded around. She took out her pocket loud speaker, turned on the microphone, and recommenced her recital from her standard script.

"Look above you and you will see the eye of the cave." Obediently we stared upwards. We saw a space, blacker than the dark roof around it, but not definite enough to be called a hole. "The 'eye' appears to form the focus of the strange and beautiful patterns which attract millions of visitors to this spot every year. We also believe that the eye listens to the wishes of the people who stand under it. If this is so, the sponsors of this expedition warn you to be careful of the wishes that you make." While we tittered our ritual laughter at the standard joke, she took out a small flute from her bag.

"Music has been found to stimulate the sympathetic centers of the cave," she said, as she lifted the flute to her mouth. "Researchers have found that the tune I will play is especially stimulating. Please close your eyes. Only in this way will you be able to achieve maximum concentration."

This is like a children's game, I thought to myself. Why should we close our eyes while she plays a tin whistle? We should look at *her* to aid our sympathetic concentration. But I decided to go along with the game; I could always peek a little.

She played a tentative first few notes on the flute. The habitual preoccupied expression on her face disappeared. She smiled. Her body seemed to lengthen and sway. When I closed my eyes, I could still see an after-image of her transfigured face.

She played the flute for several minutes, but stopped abruptly. "Now keep your eyes closed," she said, "Very tightly. Researchers believe that we now form a sort of group mind. Our power carries our wishes above to the eye of the cave and outwards to the walls." She resumed the tune.

The tune she played on the flute was so intricate and soothing that it would have charmed a whole world, let alone a solitary cave somewhere beneath the surface of this vegetable planet. My wish floated out from me tumbling end over end in the stream of the music. I could see only one image and think one thought; I wished that she might step toward me, not away from me; that she would smile at me, not look away; that her starched, silly uniform would unwrap itself from her body while she welcomed me to join with her.

A blow stung the side of my body. I fell to the floor of the cave. The mossy surface turned hard and buffeted me as I lay there. I tried to sit upright, but this time a hand seemed to hit my face. Maybe I lost consciousness for a moment, for an instant later I found myself stretched on the cave floor, which rocked violently beneath me.

Only after a few minutes of tossing on the moss did I think to open my eyes. The first people I saw clearly were the two tourists from Kansas clinging to each other. To judge from the expressions on their faces they had gained their wish to relive the pleasure of their honeymoon. Others just sat there and smiled, or gritted their teeth and grimly *wished* for some heart's desire that might be fulfilled later. The cave floor did not buffet them; only a small patch around me was still shaking.

I looked out over the cave floor, trying to see where she was. The cave had become almost too dark for me to see at a distance. Eventually I could make out her form. I walked toward her. Her body and face were still transfigured, but now she was lying full length on the floor of the cave.

I stepped toward her and stopped. What seemed like an invisible wall separated me from her. She looked up, but she was not smiling for me. She was smiling up toward the roof of the cave. I looked up, too. I saw a long silver thread begin to drop from the middle of the cave's eye. Gracefully the thread looped and danced down the wall, leapt across the floor, and stopped at her side. The end of the silver thread swelled into a large green-glowing ball which spilled up and over her body. Quickly it covered her body and throbbed. From it a rainbow of colors flashed out beacon beams bright enough to illuminate the entire cave.

My eyes were so dazzled that I closed them tightly for some time. When I opened them, I could barely see my surroundings. I stepped toward the invisible wall. It had disappeared. I ran toward her. The bulb of silver had collapsed. It withdrew from her body, and on the end of the thread, flew up toward the center of the eye of the cave. Her uniform, still looking starched and plain, was quite immaculately dry.

She lay back on the moss, looking exhausted and satisfied. I leaned over her. She opened her eyes and looked at me. I expected the cold expression to return to her face. Instead, she smiled at me. As I reached her, she grabbed at my feet and pulled me down beside her. She began to kiss my face and rumple my hair.

"Oh, Mr. Trella," she said, her voice now as joyful and welcoming as the sound of the flute she had played only a few minutes earlier. "Mr. Trella, darling, you were so wonderful!"

Stefan Vucak

Fulfilment

The grass was tall, wide and spiky. It covered the gently sloping valley. The breeze reached out in tentative fingers through the whispering grass. It hovered then whooshed across the valley. The wide blades, exposing their silvery sides, bowed after it. Tall majestic trees bordering the valley, rustled their yellowing, drying leaves after the playful tugging puffs of air. Wisps of gold, red and orange drifted down among the branches to lay a thickening carpet around the wide, gnarled trunks. High in the crown, slender branches sang with the wind, united in the slow melody.

Bubbling, hurrying water, pausing momentarily before moss and algae covered rocks, gurgled in greeting and raced merrily down the brook. A frog raised its enormous eyes above the surface of a small pool and hesitated. Crickets chattered, secure in their covering of short lush grass. A bird, all gold and fire, perched on a twig and voiced its joy.

A shadow slid quickly over the field. The wind, soaring, twisted around the lazily sunning clouds. It pushed, chased, drawing wispy snow white streamers from the glittering masses. The merest grunt of annoyance rumbled from a slumbering gray giant, sending the wind into startled erratic flight.

He lay in the grass, hands behind his head. The sky mirrored itself in the depths of his blue eyes. The muted buzzing of insects filled his ears. Chewing a blade of grass, he smiled at the antics of a butterfly flying around it. The sun, peering around branches, smiled at him, caressing his body with fingers of warmth. Creeping over his shoulder, the wind playfully swept a golden lock of hair across his eyes. He chuckled.

With a smooth flow of power, muscles rippling, he rose and spread his arms, twisting his body as he stretched. He was tall. He walked toward the brook, tingling with pleasure, sensitive to the grass beneath his feet. The frog sunning itself on the moss-covered rock croaked and jumped into the water as he knelt. He leaned until his face was just above the gurgling water, then he blew into it, watching the tiny indentation form. He blew harder. The water rose around the deeper indentation, broke and splashed against his face. His skin tingled with the cold as he drank. He stood up and looked into the valley.

The rest of the herd was slowly moving toward the forest. One of them ran from the group. Another two followed. They ended up rolling through the tall grass, flattening it into irregular clearings. Sounds of laughter drifted toward him. He grunted with content. On the far side of the valley, young ones ran shrieking around trees in their play.

A shadow drifted over him, lingered and was gone. A chill crept through his body. He shivered and looked about. He was nervous. Shouts were coming from the herd. They were running toward the forest. He saw terror contorting their faces. He started breathing rapidly. He looked at the sky and felt the hair on his head stiffen. Images from his youth flashed through his mind. He watched the first flat shapes fly toward the valley, feeling himself go pale. His pumping heart sounded loud in his ears. Thunder grumbled in the distance and rolled toward him. A flicker of lightning twisted toward the ground. Fear was new to him. He felt pain grow in his chest. He turned and ran into the forest.

He did not know where he was running. His legs, arms and chest bore raw lines inflicted by bushes and low branches. He stumbled and fell, he gave a sob as the weary muscles in his legs throbbed with pain. Then he was lying on rotting leaves. The smell of decaying vegetation was strong but not unpleasant. He rolled over on his back and breathed deeply. He shivered as his fear rose in waves and receded. The trees were around him, close. Through the branches and leaves, fire colored the sky. Yellows and reds merged as the clouds raced together. Thunder rolled over the forest, its deep voice making the ground tremble. Dusk settled quickly, drawing the cloak of darkness after it. Now he felt safe. He turned his head, listening. The hushed wind whispered through the trees. There was a crackling of leaves as of some small creature scampering around. Frogs were conducting a concert nearby. A mosquito buzzed around his head and fled when he moved. He smelt water and dampness. A drop fell, touching his face with cold. Stars winked at him. He looked at them. There were so many. He slept.

The merest breath of wind stirred the leaf. Clear tears of dawn, lamenting the passage of night, trembled and merged into one pure jewel. The teardrop slid down the leaf and hung at the tip. A fleeting ray of light, jumping from leaf to leaf, splashed itself against the drop. A rainbow flared for an instant in its heart; then the drop plummeted toward the shadowy undergrowth.

He felt the drop hit his chest, and he opened his eyes. He smiled at the deepness of the clear sky, the silent trees and the noises of life around him. The air had that sharp alive quality it always has after rain. He breathed deeply of it. He felt content.

Between the trees, he could see the plain and the hills beyond. He felt restless. His legs yearned for a run down valleys and meadows. The herd would be there. He emerged from the forest and ran through the dew-sprinkled grass, creating fleeting rainbows behind him. He ran to the top of the hill and looked around. There was no sign of the herd. He was puzzled and slightly concerned. Strange noises seemed to come from the other side of the hill. He listened. There was nothing. Maybe it was the herd. He walked uncertainly over the crest.

Four circular flat shapes were resting on the plain below. He saw what looked like a red herd moving away from the shapes as fear welled up within him. One of the red things looked at him and stopped. He was already turning to run away when he saw the creature's eyes. His whole body seemed to grow numb. His legs trembled and he stumbled backwards and fell. He was whimpering with fear as he struggled to his feet. He could feel the strange eyes staring into his back. He cried out and ran over the crest toward the welcoming forest.

He fell beside a rotting tree sprawled on the forest floor. He could run no further. He could cry no more. His lungs felt filled with thorns. It was agony for him to breathe. He ached all over. There was blood on his legs. It was bright red. It startled him. He had never seen so much blood.

He had trapped himself. There was no way out. He did not dare venture out into the open. An unbearable thirst brought with it physical pain. He remembered the brook by the forest edge. Fear rose again in his mind. Those eyes. But he could not wait for the comforting cloak of darkness to shield him while his whole body demanded water.

The forest was something he understood. As he walked toward the brook, he kept glancing back. Trees shifted strangely. Shapes formed out of the shadows. He was on the verge of panic, barely controlled. He did not feel safe any more. Dry leaves rustled behind him. He yelled in terror and ran. After a while he stopped and looked back. There was nothing unfamiliar.

He could see the swaying grass beyond the trees. Darting from one tree to another, he gradually moved closer to the bubbling brook. There was nothing threatening there. Cautiously, he emerged into the open, soaking up the warm rays from the smiling sun. He knelt beside the brook and glanced around him before submerging his face in the water. He drank and splashed the icy water on his chest and legs. After washing off the blood, he drank again. He laughed, his skin tingling with the radiant feeling of life.

The wind played with his hair. He listened to the whispering grass and the nodding, rustling branches. A dry twig snapped. He turned quickly and looked into the forest. A slim red figure stepped around from behind a tree. The figure was in shadow, yet his strange eyes burned with inner fire. They seemed to grow, drawing him.

He tried to look away, but his body refused to obey. He felt something snap and tear in his head. It hurt. He was screaming inside his head, trying to hide from the compelling eyes. Darkness welled from a corner of his mind and he welcomed its protection. But the eyes burned it into shreds, forcing him to look at the creature.

Musical sounds came from the being as it walked slowly toward him. They were soft and soothing, calming him. It was confusing. The creature looked like one of the herd. It was smaller and thinner than him. The red thing ended at the neck and wrists and did not look like skin. It stopped at arm's length. He watched the wind playing in the streaming yellow hair. The face looking at him was smiling.

Slowly it moved its slender hand to the top of the red covering. The hand moved down the center of the body and he could see skin as the covering parted. The creature stepped out of its false skin and more soothing sounds come from its mouth. He was fascinated by the false skin lying crumpled on the grass. The eyes pulled at him.

The creature's skin was light and smooth. The body was delicate. No muscles rippled beneath the skin. Two round mounds of flesh swayed as it breathed. The creature stopped smiling, reached out its hand and touched his cheek. He shuddered. Strange sensations raced through his body in quick succession. He felt hot and cold as images of sunlight, water, sky and trees burst in his mind and faded.

He felt his body slowly sink toward the grass; it brushed his legs as it swayed. The creature stood looking down at him and smiled. Its eyes flared, boring into him. A gurgle rose in his throat. He cried out as darkness shadowed the smiling creature. He felt himself falling and his mind screamed, trapped by the burning eyes.

The flat shapes were flying low over the forest. The young one ran from the tree he was hiding behind and watched the shapes grow smaller and vanish into the hazy distance. He shrieked with glee and ran toward the playing herd.

A leaf detached itself from a branch. The wind darted after it. It fluttered toward the brook, hovered above a semi-transparent figure before it settled on the face. It looked as if a patch of mist had covered the grass. Slowly, the outlines blurred and vanished. The leaf hesitated then settled itself on the moss with the grass rising around it.

Randal Flynn

Down Toward the Sun

Pluto, somewhere behind, was drifting out of range while down below the sun burned white and small reminding me of a long black well that I had seen and whose waters, far away, blazed with the reflections of my torch.

But enough of that—I have a love-story to tell you and I want you to listen. The first thing I want to say is that it isn't a love-story—not if you ask me. To me—and I should know—it is a hate-story. But she refuses to believe. She says—and I can hear her even here—that we are lovers.

Bitch.

The sun is falling closer. Each day it rises up the well a little more, looming real and awkward in my mind. I shut my eyes, I turn away, I will not watch her.

The hour will come when I am forced to stand here at the screen and see my immortality shattered in my eyes. This I dread, this I hate—even more than the hate I feel for *her*.

The Computer malfunctioned—or the displacement drive was out of kilter. I know little of machinery and when the red lights glared on the console and the alarms echoed down the mazes I was at once aware of my own vast ignorance.

So I did nothing but walk the steel corridors whose air is filled with humming and distant whirring and the muted quiver of the atomic engines far below, behind.

At night, when the lights were dimmed and the ship was

strangely hushed, I stalked the corridors, blaming Earth and the people who had sent me into space.

I cursed Haddon for his invention of the Slipspace Drive and I cursed Tramble whose idea it had been to dart toward the sun for surgravity and then wink away in the nick of time. All these I cursed, and found solace in the lack of responses.

I found her in the mess, her golden hair cradled in two warm brown arms. I stopped on the threshold and stared at her, not comprehending her existence—not there in the ship with me at that specific time.

As I stood there she stirred and raised her head and looked at me and I gasped. I knew her. Beyond a doubt I knew her and she knew me.

"How did you get in here?" My voice was far from steady.

She shook her head and said, "I don't remember. It is strange—it is as if I had never been before. And this . . . this is like my first place. And you—I recall your face. I know you, I think. Are you—?"

I nodded, almost savagely. "Yes. You and me. And you're my back-up, I suppose? They never tell me who they're sending; I never asked. Well, it doesn't matter. The mission's off."

"Mission? What—?"

"You weren't—?" Surely she had been briefed? "They must have told you something."

"No. Nothing."

Then I realized. "Of course! The computer would do that on arrival, before waking you up."

"Is the mission off because I've been awakened prematurely?"

"In a way," I said. She frowned ever so slightly and I explained about the computer and the drive and about the sun.

Her expression did not change; what her feelings were I could not tell. She did not let me in nor let herself be seen. But I knew how she felt. In fact I knew her emotions to a nuance. There was nothing she need tell me, nor I tell her. I turned on my heel and left the room—without goodbye, and without having eaten. I was no longer hungry.

She found me—if she were looking, and I knew she was—up forward on the bridge.

"No women on the bridge," I said, and gazed away from her out into space.

She took nothing of what I said and came quite close to me. Her hand rested on my arm but I shook it off.

"Don't touch me," I yelled at her. She did not change. But came toward me once again. She embraced me and I twisted away but she followed me and every time she touched me I felt a thrill of pride and revulsion. I loved her—and hated her. Needed her in this time of doom, and loathed that need. I wanted to touch her, to caress her—I would have killed her if the means had been in my hands.

How can I explain it? There was no other way. I screwed her on the bridgehead on the flat beneath the port. Then she screwed me as I sat moulded to a chair.

I ate lunch each day at twelve o'clock. This day I was alone—I thought. She entered when I had almost finished and I could see that she had cried.

An ache inside me. I knew what she was going through.

"I'm sorry I'm late," she said, her voice controlled, save for a tiny quiver.

"That's all right. Do you want me to order?"

"No, no, please." She looked apologetic. "I'm very fussy," she explained.

And then we looked at each other and began to laugh.

"All right—go ahead. If you don't know what I like then I guess nobody does."

I ordered.

Her meal popped up through a slot in the table and she began to eat. Halfway through the meal she stopped, a spoon poised on the edge of her lips, and gazed at me abstractedly.

"You hate me," she said.

It was not a question.

"No," I said, lying for some obscure reason. "I don't."

"I love you," she said, as if it were the same thing.

Love?

Is that all?

Did that single reversed chromosome, the one that made her woman, have no hate?

"You hate me," she said again.

I nodded now, not feeling strong enough to lie. "Yes, I hate you."

"You hate yourself?"

I stared at her. Did I hate myself?

I said, "Look at that mole on your left elbow." She did and I rolled up my sleeve beyond my elbow and pointed to my mole.

"It's the same," I said.

"Of course," she replied. And further said, "We are the same."

Some time went by and I began to fill with anger.

"No, you're wrong. We're not the same. We may look alike, but I am no more you than I am Peter Havak."

She kept a stony silence.

"I'm me—alone," I reminded her.

"But I'm me, too, and we're together!"

"No. No! We'll always be alone."

"Even now?"

"Especially now. Until we reach the sun."

"Why?"

"Damme! Because we're the same—and when I'm *with* myself I'm by myself."

"You've just contradicted your*self.*"

I slapped her, and suddenly her love gushed out at me in a madness.

I hopped back, taken by surprise at the awful change in her. She reminded me of myself and her hate was something to see. I was like stone against her. The more hateful she got the harder grew my armor. But it did not last long. She simmered and cooled and gradually grew quiet.

She comes to me every night and slips into my bed beside me. I screw her and tell her how much I loathe her.

Peter—smooth and soft and warm. I love her, the bitch.

Her haughty shoulders straight and squared, her arrogant chin jutting just so, her posture so upright and perfect.

Does she know that I can't keep my hands from her, or my thoughts? I know she does? Who better than I?

"He's dead," I said. "He's been dead, Peter, for twenty-six years. You and I are lingering shadows, soon to be snuffed out."

"He's not dead," she said. "That was the whole purpose of the cloning. To preserve the better men if something happened to the originals. And now all these years of work and empiric data—and the mission—must be blanked out by the sun."

"The real Peter Havak is dead," I repeated, more firmly.

"*Real?* Then who are we? What are we?"

I shrugged. "I don't know. I can't tell you."

Walls of stainless steel rising smooth-gray-seamless from the floor. Lights that will shine on until the sun engulfs them in greater light. Engines that will hum on until they turn to vapor. Earth is behind us, and Venus and Mercury. Sol is ahead.

She is sleeping. It will be her last sleep before we hit the sun. I am in the engine room debating with myself the pros and cons of jumping into the mass convertor.

Perhaps I will.

Perhaps I won't.

Do you love yourself? It seems to me you must if you are to maintain your center and security.

Because, as I have seen, loving cancels out hating, and lets you get on with living.

Peter and I—we are both images of that long dead Peter Havak whose chromosomes, one X one Y, have finally come together, merging themselves on the bridge of a doomed spaceship.

Do you love yourself?

I do—I also hate her sometimes.

I am afraid. I am up here on the bridge alone. She waits for me in our room. She thinks that I am going to return before the end. Perhaps I will.

The sun fills all the port; the polarizers whine. The ship is very quiet. I am very much alone.

Except for myself.

Andrew Whitmore

Afterword

It was all Ursula Le Guin's fault. I want that clearly understood. She tried to lay the blame with Harlan Ellison, who invented this particular assignment, along with the Chinese Water Torture, the Death of a Thousand Cuts and other workshopping techniques. Well, perhaps he did, but it was Ursula who uttered those terrifying words:

"I want you to write a love-story."

Groans. Gasps. Sighs. "Write a what?" Insane laughter. Tears. But that lady has a heart of stone. She smiled.

And so we had a night in which to write ourselves a love-story.

That night we retired to our respective typewriters and fell to gloomy contemplation. Somehow, the idea came to me that I should attempt to write this story without using any adjectives or adverbs. (Ursula had suggested that we might like to attempt this as another assignment later on, if we had time.) All agreed that this was a most difficult project, and, thus gratified, I set about it at once.

Smart fellow!

Some difficulties presented themselves almost immediately. I found that I was remarkably ignorant as to what was and what was not an adverb. Or anything else, for that matter. At frequent intervals I would disturb the frantic silence of the room with such impassioned cries as: "Is 'under' an adverb?"

Take, for example, these two rather innocuous looking sentences:

"Nothing intrudes upon the river. There are no rocks in the water, no fallen branches."

Writing them cost me considerable time and effort.

Nothing. What is "nothing"? A noun I suppose. What intrudes upon the river? Nothing intrudes upon the river. That makes it the object. Or the subject. Something. Is it an adverb? Can an adverb be a subject? What does it say in the dictionary? God, it can be anything. Okay, it'll do. Intrudes. Yeah, that's all right. I think. Leave it anyway. Upon. Hell, that looks bad. Let me see. A verb is a doing word. Upon. Definitely not a verb. An adjective is a what? A describing word. Correct. He was upon. That doesn't sound right. What's an adverb, for Christ's sake? It describes something. The verb? Who knows. That's about as far as it goes. What else is there. Prepositions. What are they? This is ridiculous. What does it say in the dictionary? Where is my dictionary? All right, who took my dictionary? Oh, here it is. Let me see. Up. Upas. Upbraid. Upon. Well, look at that. Great. There, one sentence already. You're smarter than you look. Here we go. There. Right. Are. Verb, yeah. No. Ah. I see. No. Urk. Let's face it, Andrew, things are not working out. No. What does it say in the dictionary?

It didn't get any easier.

By some miracle, I managed to complete one paragraph, and I would stare at this with a kind of lunatic joy, before tearing the paper from the typewriter in frustration when an adverb insinuated itself into the next sentence and so ruined everything.

I began to think that every word in the English language was an adverb of some denomination or the other or, if not, then the dictionary I consulted was, in fact, no dictionary at all, but rather some devilish torment devised to punish anyone audacious enough to attempt to write a love-story without using adjectives or adverbs.

I spent all night in this occupation. I would type out a paragraph, sit staring at the typewriter for half an hour or so, watching the little black words swirling about on the white paper, and then I would tear the page out, replacing it with a new sheet with which I repeated this strange ritual.

No one seemed to observe this rather futile pastime of mine and, one by one, they departed my company. David Grigg paced me for a while, and I darted looks of pure hatred at him as he completed one page after the other, pulling sheets of paper from his typewriter, not because an insidious adverb compelled him to do so, but so that he could get on with his story. After a time (somewhere near 3 A.M.: the night was but young) he, too, departed my company, having completed his story. I was left to suffer my torment alone.

Next morning I had a sheaf of paper about two inches thick on the table beside me. Each sheet contained virtually the same thing. True, I had somehow managed to add two paragraphs to the original one, but they were hardly large, and the total word count was something less than sixty. And even then I wouldn't swear to God that there wasn't an adverb or two lurking in there somewhere.

When I heard people moving about, I hastily hid this large amount of incriminating evidence, and wandered over with the others for breakfast.

That day was passed in a kind of stupor. The events that occurred are not clear to me, nor are my actions. (Bruce Gillespie, however, has kindly preserved for posterity some of my more inane statements.)

Like Dante, I was midway through my allotted span, and, as with him, I was pretty much lost. But I was far from defeated. That night I recommenced my labors with renewed (well...) vigor.

It slowly occurred to me that I was making no real progress with this story (yes, it did). Sometime after midnight I decided that things were getting serious. I had to have a story for the workshopping session the next day. That's what the whole thing was about.

Fortunately, just as I realized that typing out the same four paragraphs over and over again wasn't going to produce much in the way of workshopping material, I had an IDEA.

Now this was rather remarkable for me. I do not usually produce ideas at any fantastic rate. Some people at the workshop tossed off ideas as if they were nothing, but ideas come to me slowly and infrequently. Yet, there I was, in the small hours of the morning, with an idea that was spitting and snarling to get out.

All at once I had a plot, a form, characters, the lot. Even so, it took some time to get it all down on paper. I knew what I wanted to say, but somewhere between my head and the typewriter things kept getting distorted. Sometimes it took half an hour to write one sentence. Work was not made any easier by the intrusion of a number of hallucinatory beings who persisted in whispering incoherently, looking over my shoulder and generally acting in a distracting and annoying manner.

I soon decided that the story was perhaps the best ever written. The style and approach were original (I thought) and effective. I remember laughing hysterically when the title came to me, because I saw at once how perfect it was, even if A.E. van Vogt did use it first. (Admittedly, I had been laughing hysterically, if softly, at random intervals for a good many hours.)

Despite these difficulties, I did finish the story. When I had put down the last words, I returned to the first page and typed boldly on the top:

PROCESS
(4.35 a.m.)

I then took the page from the typewriter and stapled all four pages of the story together. When this was done, I systematically destroyed every trace of the story: any piece of paper that had the slightest connection with it, from rough drafts to pieces of scribbled dialogue. I tore these pieces of paper into minute fragments and buried them deep in the rubbish bin.

Paranoia satisfied, I placed another piece of paper in the typewriter and wrote a brief, yet poignant note, which perhaps gives a better impression of my condition than any retrospective article written seven months later.

I left this note sitting in the typewriter and went upstairs to bed, taking extreme pains to secrete the manuscript where no one could find it but me.

Next day I awoke feeling relatively alive. I put on my dressing-gown and stumbled downstairs. On encountering something that resembled a human being I enquired reasonably: "What time is it?" which seemed to be highly amusing. I was informed that it was three o'clock. Well, well.

I duplicated copies of my story and then joined the rest of the group in the main building for a workshopping session.

The story *Process* was duly workshopped. Ursula's first comment was: "Perhaps you have to have been awake until 4:35 A.M.

to appreciate this story." Her concluding comment was: "It's not a love story."

In fact, no one seemed to understand the story at all. I agreed that it was rather different, but I considered everyone to be remarkably ignorant not to appreciate the enormous power and pathos of the story. Looking back over it now I find it . . . Well, never mind.

I was later informed that the story was 270 words long, and that I had been awake for something like 45 hours straight before finishing it. It was calculated that this was an average of six words for every hour awake. I haven't checked these figures, but they give one food for thought.

"This is being typed as the time approaches 5 A.M. Some strange things are going on in this room. For example, whenever I stop and listen, I can hear a babble of voices (Pip's voice is especially clear). There also seem to be recognizable human figures scattered around the room. I only see them out of the corner of my eye, but they are very distinct. At this very moment Robert Young is doing something over at the sink, and Derrick Ashby is over there somewhere, too. Randal also appears quite regularly, usually mulling over a manuscript. (Robert sometimes looks over my shoulder as I write.) All this is hardly pleasant. (Fortunately, Randal is silent, which keeps the situation from becoming unbearable.)

I would like all this to be borne in mind when my story is workshopped. (And it won't be workshopped until I wake up, whatever the hour, because I have the manuscript.)

I wish Derrick would get out of it. I can see him plain as day.

Unfortunately, the voices have come back, with Randal's prominent.

I am going to bed.

If I do not wake again it will probably be too soon.

ANDREW WHITMORE

THE DIALOGUES

With the Dialogues we were forced to think about Character: we couldn't use names to identify man or woman, so what makes one series of words sound appropriate to a man, and another series appropriate to a woman? Perhaps there is no difference. Or is there?

We thought about stereotypes, about male chauvinist pigs and female chauvinist sows, and about people as real as we could remember. Our dialogues covered the whole range.

Of the four examples here, Andrew Whitmore's was actually written as his Love Story (so was Annis Shepherd's *Duplicates*)—but as you have probably noticed, good stories can fit into many different categories.

Rob Gerrand

Andrew Whitmore

Process

SHE: Hello, Jay.
    Hello.
SHE: Do you like this place, Jay?
    Alone.
SHE: I'm here, Jay.
    Yes.
SHE: You like me being here, don't you, Jay?
    Yes.
SHE: So you don't mind being alone?
    Dark.
SHE: You're not afraid of the dark, are you? Not someone big and
    strong like you.
    No.
SHE: Of course you're not.
    Strong.
SHE: Yes, you're very strong, Jay.
    Strong.
SHE: It's good to be strong, isn't it, Jay?
    Good.
SHE: If you're strong, then you don't have to be afraid of anything. I
    bet you're not afraid of anything.
    No.
SHE: I didn't think you would be. You're too strong. But do you
    know something, Jay? *I* get frightened sometimes.
    ☐
SHE: Do you know why?
    No.

SHE: Because of the Enemy.
□

SHE: You know who the Enemy are, don't you, Jay?
Yes.

SHE: Do you know what they do?
They kill.

SHE: That's right—they kill. And that's why I am frightened.
□

SHE: Unless they are stopped they will kill me.
You.

SHE: Yes, Jay. They will kill me.
□

SHE: If I were killed, I couldn't talk to you anymore.
No.

SHE: Would you like that, Jay?
No.

SHE: Neither would I. I...I like to talk to you, Jay.
□

SHE: Do you understand why I get so frightened sometimes?
Yes.

SHE: No one can do anything.
Yes.

SHE: What do you mean? Who can help me, Jay?
Jay.

SHE: But how?
Kill.

SHE: You mean...you will kill the Enemy?
Yes.

SHE: There are a lot of the Enemy, Jay.
Kill.

SHE: Would you do that for me, Jay?
Yes.

SHE: Why?
□

SHE: Thank you, Jay. I never thought that anyone would ever...
□

SHE: Thank you.
Kill.

SHE: Yes, Jay, kill the Enemy. That will make me very happy. Kill.

SHE: I'm sorry, Jay. You'll have to go now. I didn't realize we had been talking so long. I'll try and see you again soon. Goodbye, Jay.
Goodbye.

SHE: Hello, Kay.

John Edward Clark

It's Not Too Late

A: Here. Take it.

B: I don't know.

A: Take it. There's no alternative.

B: I don't know.

A: Look. We've been all over this before. We have to face facts. It'll take the rescue ship six hours to get here. There's only three hours of oxygen left for each of us. One of us has to die so that the other can live. It's as simple as that. Face it.

B: I'm scared. I'm really scared.

A: Look. This is the only fair way. We flipped a coin, and you lost, so you're first turn. Take the gun ... Take it!

B: Shut up, just shut up! ... here, give it to me.

A: No, hold it up higher.

B: Shut up.

A: Point it downwards.

B: Shut up!

A: Squeeze it slowly.

B: SHUT UP ...

I know how to blow my own head off.

(pause)

Click

(pause)

Here ... your turn.

A: You know I was seventeen when I first joined the service. I remember ...

B: Take it.

A: I remember my first assignment. It was a disciplinary mission to
   the rebel planet Thar. I was really raw. I nearly blew it. We were
   flying low in the atmosphere, you see, and the Captain turned to
   me and said, "Push the button."
   I was daydreaming. I didn't hear him. "Push the button you," he
   growled. "Button, button, what button, Sir?" I asked.
   "The red one!" he growled. I was really embarrassed. I felt such a
   fool. I pushed the button. I found out later I'd destroyed a city of
   five million people. I don't regret it. I don't regret any of it. I was
   doing my duty.

B: Here's the gun.

A: I don't regret any of it.
   (pause)
   Click
   (pause)
   Phew!

B: A family, that's what I miss most. My own kids. I never had any.
   Why? I don't know why. I should have. It's too late now. I've been
   stupid, so stupid. And it's too late.

A: Hurry up.

B: How did I ever get into this mess? I've been stupid. So stupid. And
   it's too late.

A: Pull it.
   (pause)
   Click
   (pause)

B: God.

A: Shit.

B: H...here.

A: Ha ha. I've been a gambler all my life... I've bet on dice and
   cards, and wheels... everything... ha ha... a gambler... I don't
   regret any of it... Goodbye.
   (pause)
   Click

B: My God. My God. My God.
   (pause)

B: Fffflowers... my m-mother's got ro-ses in her garden... beautiful roses... and... marigolds... an... grass... green grass... I

love that garden...Jesus...I love my mother...you know...I don't think I ever t-told her I love her. I've be-be-been so stupid...I should have got married a long time ago...I c-could have...but I didn't...and now it's too late...too late...good-bye.

A: Goodbye.

(pause)

Bang.

(long pause)

B: I had to do it...I had to...I had to...I've been a loser all my life...I had to do it...I had to...I've never had a family of my own...I've been stupid...so stupid...But it's not too late.

Bruce Barnes

After the Wreck of
The *Stellar Queen*

A: Uh... we're making this recording just before re-entering Earth's atmosphere. Our lifeboat has no radio, so we're using the flight-log...just in case anything goes wrong. Not that I expect anything *will* go wrong, honey.

B: I don't see how anything could go wrong, darling. This craft belongs to your father's company, doesn't it?

A: Uh...yeah. But so did the *Stellar Queen*...

B: Oh, don't be so gloomy, darling. Let's cheer ourselves up and announce our engagement...formally?

A: Well, I would rather wait until we're sure how we both feel. Remember the story I told you, the one about the sailor on the old-time sailing ship who fell in love with the first female face he saw, after a year at sea? Now I know it's only been three months since the *Queen* blew up...but, well, you know what I mean.

B: I think three months is quite long enough for two people to get to know each other as well as we do, darling. Don't you?

A: It isn't the same for me. I'm twice as old as you and...I've never been married before.

B: Not even *once?*

A: No.

B: Well, I can assure you it's nothing to be afraid of, dearest, I've been married *six* times...

A: Look, do you mind if we change the subject—at least while this machine is running? You're making my ears go—

B: Listen—did you hear that?

A: Oh, that—that's the air friction. We've entered the atmosphere.

B: Oh, don't look so glum, darling. We're almost *home!* Isn't it

144

exciting! There will be so many things for us to see and do—please don't look so glum. Just think of all the places we can visit . . . together. So many places I'm dying to show you, so many wonderful people I want you to meet . . .

A: Uh-oh.

B: Uh-oh?

A: There's . . . something I forgot to mention. The *Stellar Queen* had only six lifeboats. All the time I've been wondering if we picked *that* one. Now I know we did: those flashing red lights on the control panel prove it.

B: I don't quite understand, darling.

A: Those hot-cold separator thingamies: the ones that stop a ship burning up when it enters the atmosphere . . .

B: The Maxwell Demons?

A: Yeah, them. This boat doesn't have any. A few days before the explosion I, well, you know how curious I am about mechanical things—and seeing as how my father's company makes them and all—I figured I should try and learn a little more about them. You know how it is. I . . . I'm really sorry I got us into this mess, honey. It's really my fault that we won't—

B: Why, you stupid bloody fool! *You knew all this time?* Why, you feeble-minded, grong-brained—

A: But honey! Look, wait a moment—

B: You moron! It's all your fault. Oh, why did I ever have to get mixed up with you? You fat old—

A: Can it, honey. Hear that buzzing? That's the Demons coming on. The reason the red lights were flashing is because I changed the wiring around a few weeks ago.

B: You . . . *what?*

A: Changed the wiring. After all, a guy likes to make sure how his partner *really* feels before he commits himself to matrimony. If you know what I mean.

Ursula K. Le Guin

No Use to Talk to Me

A: I don't think there's anything we can do.

B: Where's the Handbook?

A: There... right there, in its place. But, you know, we've tried everything the—

B: All right, all right, just be quiet a minute, will you? The back-up system... Where's the diagram?

A: Page eighty.

B: Eighty. Right. All right. There has to be some way to reconnect...

Page eighty, all right, here it is.

Right. (long pause; mumbling)... connect Lead A5 to the injector line—but for Christ's sake! all the damned leads are fused; how do they expect me to connect bloody A5 Lead when there isn't any bloody A5 lead any more! (pause) What are you doing?

A: Putting the Handbook back.

B: Oh, that's right. Keep the Handbook in its place. Keep the ship neat and tidy at all times. Very important. When it's all going to smash to bloody bits in half an hour! For Christ's sake stop wasting time and keep trying to raise Ground Control. Don't you realize we have to get a signal through?

A: We can't. We can't send. The short-out—

B: Will you just stop talking and try to get that signal through?

A: The transmitter's set on automatic. If a signal were going out they'd be receiving. I think—

B: Take it off auto! Use the manual! Don't you understand, we *have* to get through? Switch it over to my mike. Control, Control,

146

Control, this is Scout Two, do you read me, this is Scout Two, Control, do you read me? Control, this is Scout Two, this is Scout Two, do you read me? Control—

A: Please don't.

B: This is Scout Two. We have a serious emergency, do you read me? Control—

A: Please don't.

B: Listen! If we don't get through, if we don't get help, we're coming down like a Goddamned meteorite, don't you understand that?

A: If we did make radio contact there's nothing they could do. Except say goodbye.

B: They might be able to... They could... There has to be something... Control, Control, this is Scout Two, this is Scout Two... All right. All right. So what do we do?

A: I don't know, Maybe we...

B: We what?

A: Maybe we say goodbye.
   (Pause)

B: Yeah. All right. I guess... Yeah.

A: It was a good trip, wasn't it?

B: It was one hell of a good trip. From the start. (Pause) Listen, I never was any good at goodbyes and stuff.

A: I know. Neither was I.

B: You've got the radio on auto, don't you?

A: Yeah.

B: When I was a kid, when I was really scared about something coming up, like at the dentist, you know, I used to recite things to myself.

A: What kind of things?

B: Anything. Anything I'd memorized. Poetry, the multiplication tables, you know.

A: I'm game.

B: Twelve times eight—?

A: I never could do twelves. How about... Wait... "When I was one and twenty, I heard a wise man say—"

B: "Give crowns and pounds and pennies, But not your heart away."

A: Guineas.

B: What?

A: Guineas, not pennies.
B: Is it? All right;
A&B:
    "Give crowns and pounds and guineas,
    But not your heart away.
    Give pearls away and rubies,
    But keep your fancy free."
A: "But I was one and twenty,
    No use to talk to me..."

Duplication of Effort

The workshop submission stories were copied well in advance, and by the time we had finished those I estimated that we had already used up something like a quarter of the useful life of the machine we had hired. And by the end of the workshop we would clock up about another 10,000 copies: about 1500 per day.

Getting the copier to Booth Lodge presented us with some problems. I was happy to be able to hitch a ride together with the machine I had been taking care of, but unfortunately no one had given us any instructions as to how to get the beast into "transport" mode. Later in the week, I discovered a means of moving it around without leaving a trail of ink all over the floor, but for the moment the best we could do was to manhandle the copier on to the footpath, upend it, and let the ink flow out into the gutter. When it was clean and empty, we loaded it into Peter Darling's Volvo. By now an interested crowd had gathered to watch our antics. We had to offload some luggage to get the copier in, then repack it around the machine: it would be a long, winding drive up to Booth Lodge. And it was only when we arrived at the end of our forty-mile journey that I realized I had left my bags behind on the front porch! At least I had my typewriter.

Bruce Gillespie had recurring nightmares beforehand about the photocopying of material produced during the workshop. I believe he had visions of being stuck in a tiny room at the Lodge, kept busy passing out copies of stories through a narrow slot in the wall, while someone else kept passing him in manuscripts and food through another. But as it turned out, everyone did most of their own copying. Stories were finished and copied at all hours of day and night, and this was much easier than having to do them all in one batch. There were only two paper jams during the week, and I shudder to think of how many times the ink reservoir was re-filled. If anyone reading this is thinking of running a workshop along similar lines I have one important suggestion—use a dry copier! But there were really no problems that could not be overcome by whoever was using the machine at the time.

And Bruce Gillespie even found time to write some fiction.

DERRICK ASHBY

THE WORD GAMES

After the softening up process of writing the "single change" stories—such a weird feeling we had: we now felt that, could it be, yes, perhaps...perhaps our wild dreams and hopes were not so wild. Hell, we seemed to be able to produce the most bizarre, exciting, crazy, *fantastic* ideas. What would we do next? We were bubbling with enthusiasm. No time for false modesty, no time for lack of confidence.

And Ursula gave us the Word Game: what better way to let our burgeoning, curious imaginations expand and grow? Each of us picked at random a piece of paper from two piles, and thus obtained an adjective and a noun around which to write a story. Orgy. Healing. Those were my lucky ones. Healing Orgy. The images that immediately jumped to mind! Wilhelm Reich, where are you? But this gift of Healing and Orgy is far too precious to be thrown away.

Each of us, as you will see, was unable to take the easy way out. We all wrestled with our pairs of words, pacing up and down, stretching and twisting our hair, sitting in blankness, suddenly typing furiously, emitting exuberant yells, emitting despairing moans. Around 3 a.m. it was a little difficult to get to sleep, what with all the adrenalin and elation, and trepidation.

ROB GERRAND

Pip Maddern

Broken Pit

There were seven of them crawling, one behind the other, up the stony airshaft. They were all carrying loads of miscellaneous filched goods. Filek went first because the whole idea was his; he carried on his back a small square package of the precious bang-crash stuff. Mosil dragged a pick, and an assortment of shoring boards. Seim and Diak had packets of food (crusts and scraps they had collected over many hungry days), dried mushroom spores, and some more shoring boards. Garm carried two shovels on his shoulder. They were heavy, and kept slipping. His left hand flickered nervously between the shovels and the rock floor of the shaft, keeping the shovels, and himself in proper balance. Wiken and Hom propelled a little ore-carrying trolley between them. Wiken pulled, and Hom pushed. It was hard work, and they made a good deal of noise over it, arguing in whispers as the wheels clanged and wrenched at the stones on the steep slope. Periodically the whole line would take fright, and a ripple of shushing would pass up and down the shaft. They would all be silent for a minute or two, listening, fearing that the Flying Giants might be following them. Then, slowly, timidly, they would start forward again, slipping, muttering and whispering toward the Top.

The shaft was dark, but the end showed as a star-shaped grayness. When he reached the edge, Filek stopped, hesitated, dithered. The six behind him cannoned into each other, with varying degrees of scuffle and confusion. Garm dropped one of his shovels. Filek put his right foot out, and withdrew it quickly. Then he peered out cautiously round the edge of the hole. The air smelt sharp and strange and terrifying, but at least there was none of the rank smell of the Flying Giants.

Greatly daring, he put out his foot, and set it on the ground outside. There was something soft and squashy there, but he could feel the good solid rock underneath. He stood for a moment, awkwardly straddling the lip of the hole. Then, in a burst of courage, he ducked his head and ran a few steps into the open. In a panic, Mosil and Seim and Diak crowded after him. Garm scrabbled frantically for his shovel, found it, and leaped out. Wiken and Hom got the trolley stuck on the lip of the hole, and bickered in furious whispers, straining and heaving and hindering each other.

Mosil ran back to help, and between them, with a final echoing clang, they tipped the trolley out. Then they all froze, listening. The night was full of rustles and creaks and the tiny complaining voices of bats. They shivered and cowered at the new noises.

Far away, there was a little mound of lights. Filek said, ducking his head away from the horrible arching space above him, "That's the Flying Giants' tunnel."

The others looked at him with respect. Filek should know. Filek was the foreman of their digging group. He had once had to go to the Flying Giants to explain why the group had dug out so few shiny-stones one week. Filek had thought of them digging their way out of their tunnel to the airshaft. Filek was brave. They waited to see what he would do next.

Filek turned away from the lights of the Flying Giants' tunnel, and set off down the side of the mountain. His convoy shook itself into an approximation of order, and followed him. The stuff underfoot was messy and slippery. Soon they were going much faster than they wanted. Hom lost his grip on the trolley, which ran on relentlessly, pushing Wiken downward. Wiken and the trolley bumped into Seim. There was a confused rush, and the three of them fell into a small hollow on the side of the mountain, with Wiken underneath. He wailed protestingly. Seim shushed him without effect, until Garm appeared, and cuffed him quiet. Hom arrived, and they manhandled the trolley until it fell off Wiken. Wiken sat up, grumbling. There was a moment's pause, and then Filek and Mosil and Diak came slipping over the edge of the hollow. By common consent, they all squatted down, and rested.

After a while, Diak began to whimper. "I want to go back, I want to go back."

"We can't." (Seim)

"No, we can't." (Hom and Wiken, overlapping)

"The Flying Giants—"

"They make us dig—"

"Well, we like digging but—"

"They make us dig every day."

"Why can't we dig when we like?"

"They make us dig—"

"They like our shiny-stones."

"Well, I like their bang-crash stuff." (Garm)

"We never used to dig like that—"

"And Filek said—"

"Never, not for a long long time back."

"And Filek said we could—"

"But the Flying Giants don't like rock—"

"Filek said we—"

"They only like shiny-stones."

"Filek said we could"

"Ssh!"

"—run away."

They stopped, and peered round. The sky was growing paler and paler, seeming bigger and bigger. On the side of the trolley the black marks started to separate themselves from their background. They made a long pattern: EXTRA-TERRAN MINING CO. Looking at the trolley steadied them. They were reminded of what they had fled from. Filek said quickly. "We go."

And so they ran, with inefficient hurry, down the outside of their mountain.

At nightfall they halted again, stiff and sore, their eyes red from the unaccustomed sunshine. They were all very hungry, for they had not once dared to stop and eat all day. They were far out into the plain.

"I want to sleep," said Diak.

"Well, sleep then." (Filek)

"I want to sleep in a tunnel."

"You can't." (Seim)

"But there must be a tunnel!" (Diak, panic-stricken)

"Filek says there isn't one." (Mosil)

"We like tunnels—" (Wiken and Hom, in unison)

"But Filek says—"

"Well *I'm* going to sleep anyway." (Garm)

"—there isn't one."

"I want one." (Diak, muttering)

They slept uneasily through the night, stirring and whimpering in their sleep, clinging insecurely to the Top.

The next day, they ate some food (squashy, and warm, and not very nice, now) and set out again. They were still carrying their bundles, but Mosil dragged his pick slower and slower, and Garm kept dropping his shovels. They trailed on, arguing in whispers, glancing over their shoulder. Their mountain looked blue behind them now, but no Flying Giants came chasing them over the plain. Garm got his shovels entangled in Seim's shoring boards, and dropped them angrily.

He said loudly, "I'm not carrying them any more. I'm tired."

"Sh-sh-sh-sh-sh-sh." (The whole line)

"Well I'm not—" (Garm, but more muted)

"You have to. I have to carry my shoring boards." (Seim)

"But there's no tunnel." (Diak)

"And Filek says—"

"Well I'm not—"

"He's right, there's no tunnel—"

"Well, we have to take the trolley—"

"—tell you I'm not—"

"Wait!" said Filek.

The others hushed, gathered in an expectant circle round him.

Filek thought. He said slowly, "If all our things were shiny-stones, we could put them in the trolley."

A pause. Then—

"But they're not—"

"We have to take the trolley,"

"But we could—"

"It's not fair, we have to take the trolley."

"But Filek's right, we could—"

"Well I'm not carrying them—"

"And there *isn't* a tunnel—"

"Filek's *right,* I say, we could—"

"But they're not—"

"—put them in the trolley."

Filek said, "If we put our stuff in the trolley, we can all take turns pushing and pulling, instead of just Wiken and Hom."

Wiken and Hom looked mutinous, but Garm slung his shovels in with relief, and the rest piled their things in too. The shoring boards balanced uneasily on top. They all moved off again. Hom pulling, Garm pushing, Filek and Mosil leading, and Seim and Diak coming behind to pick up the shoring boards, which fell off very frequently.

At the next halt, Diak began to whimper again, and would not be hushed. "I'm scared, I want my tunnel," he said over and over again. The others fussed round him and patted him on the back, and ruffled his hair, and cuffed him, but it made no difference. "I want my tunnel."

Filek stood and thought. "We've got our tools..." he said.

"Yes, and they're heavy—"

"We have to push the trolley almost all the time."

("I want my tunnel, I want my tunnel, I want my tunnel.")

"You don't I do a lot—"

"We picked up the shoring boards all day—"

"Shut up!" said Filek loudly.

They all stopped and stared at him. Filek felt braver and braver. He stood up straight for the first time. He said, still loudly, "Diak wants a tunnel. We all want a tunnel, well we'll *make* a tunnel. Here."

A flurry of noise broke out. Above it, Garm could be heard saying in puzzlement, "But there's no mountain here."

"Yes, and no rock—"

("I want my tunnel.")

"Filek says—"

"We'll dig it here," said Filek.

And they did.

Once the tunnel was started, they all felt happier. They knew how to dig. It felt home-like, even though they had to take the green stringy stuff off the top and burrow through messy soft stuff underneath. But it was quick. Quite soon they had a deep pit, taller than Mosil, who was taller than the rest of them. The messy stuff fell in little dribbles to the floor of the pit, but they scooped it up again, and shored the edges well, and dug on.

That night Filek let Diak and Wiken and Hom sleep in the hole. Seim wanted to go too, but there was no room. Garm said proudly, "*We're* not afraid to sleep on Top," and after that Seim kept quiet.

The next day they dug more methodically, their first eagerness and relief over. They squared the sides nicely, and let themsleves up and down with the rope from Seim's foodpack. Garm held the end on top, bacause he was the strongest. Toward afternoon, they started a side passage out from the hole, but very soon they ran into a large, hard rock.

Mosil came up to tell Filek and Garm, who were moving the mullock pile back from the mouth of the hole. Garm said, "We can use the bang-crash stuff." He sounded pleased. Filek said, "Are you sure you can't pick-axe it out?" and Mosil said he was. "Then we will use the bang-crash stuff," said Filek.

Mosil went down the pit again to call up Wiken and Hom and Seim and Diak. Garm went down to have a look at the rock. They all discussed it. Filek got his bang-crash pack and fuse and plunger from the trolley. He made everyone stand behind the mullock heap. Then he went down the pit and scrabbled around the rock, laying the charge. He was very proud. He was the only one of the group who knew how to use the bang-crash stuff. The bang-crash stuff was the only good thing the Flying Giants had brought with them. He went back to the main pit, and shouted for Garm to pull him up. He set the plunger, and counted all the others very carefully, three times. Then he went down the hole again to make sure no one was there. Then he came up again, and ordered everyone farther back. Then he pressed down the plunger.

With a giant roar and crash, the hole burst up to the sky. Great chunks of rock showered among them, and mounds of dust slid and jumped toward what had once been their pit. For a long time, they lay flat to the ground, waiting for the muttering and groaning of the earth to die away.

One by one, they gathered round the great dust bowl, and stared silently into it. A piece of shattered shovel blade poked out of the wreckage.

Diak began to sob.

"It's broken, it's broken, it's all broken, it's gone," he gasped out, "our pit's broken, our tunnel's broken—"

Wiken said angrily to Garm, "Now look what your silly bang-crash stuff has done!" He was half-crying himself. Garm said, "I didn't do it, it was Filek who—"

"Filek didn't mean—"

"It's broken—"

"We can't—"

"And all our tools have gone—"

"We dragged that trolley—"

"Our pit's—"

"Well, Filek said—"

"He didn't mean—"

"SHUT UP!" roared Filek.

In the sudden silence, only Diak snuffled on.

Filek squared his shoulders. He made his mouth behave itself. "All right," he said, "our pit's broken. Well, we'll think of something else."

Rob Gerrand

The Healing Orgy

"Step up! Step up! Right here folks, for Baron de Quincy's one and only genuine Healing Orgy. No matter what ails you—and brothers and sisters, I can tell just by looking at you that something ails you, yes something ails you all—no matter the specific ailment, whether despondency, depression or despair, laxity, languor or laziness, hesitance, hysteria or hatred. Be it bewilderment, bashfulness—or boredom: the Healing Orgy will help.

"Just step right up folks, the Healing Orgy will put a spark in your eye, a lift in your step, lead in your pencil, hope in your heart.

"Step here, folks, it's cheap at any price."

The spruiker, fiftyish, fat and cheerful, retired briefly behind a flap of his marquee to take a swig from a bottle.

A small crowd, attracted by the spiel, stood expectantly, waiting to see who would be first to enter.

"Junior!" called a woman. "Come away at once!"

"Aw gee, mom," the urchin whined, but, with the help of a slap, came away nevertheless.

Rick had been watching from across the square, and now he moved to join the group. As he approached, the spruiker reappeared, followed by an olive-skinned girl dressed in a bikini.

The girl had an extraordinary delicacy and beauty, and she smiled tenderly, a personal searching gaze that promised delight so poignant that Rick felt his innermost being touched and opening to her.

Exhilarated, he stared at her face, drinking in her perfection. He, or the crowd, groaned in some inner anguish. High cheek bones lay

159

under dark pensive eyes. Her lips, gently sculptured like a purple-red rose, were pursed in a sweet and ironic smile.

She slowly turned and gracefully reentered the tent.

The image of her slender back, her hips and moving buttocks, etched themselves in Rick's mind.

Watching the crowd shrewdly, the spruiker repeated his phrases.

"Step up sir, step up. An experience you are unlikely to forget. Baron de Quincy assures it!"

Rick walked forward.

"Ah, I see we have one young man here, with more wisdom than most. And you sir, you madam, will you know our gifts?"

Others followed Rick, and paid their money to a beautiful youth—surely the brother of the girl.

Inside, sitting on soft red cushions, Rick noticed other men and girls from the village, and saw that they too appeared dazed and expectant.

The sides of the tent were draped in burnt orange silk. A stage was assembled before them. A heavy sweet perfume invaded Rick's nostrils.

He grew drowsy, drooped against a girl, his head falling to her knee, the girl's torso resting on Rick's shoulder. He struggled to keep his eyes open.

Looking up from his odd angle, he saw movement on the stage: strange silvery devices were wheeled in front of them. The exquisite couple appeared and seemed to glide to the front, and quietly regarded their audience. The audience barely responded. Rick seemed to have pins and needles through all his limbs, his mind seemed unattached, disinterested and no longer sleepy.

Dully he saw the girl approach one of the silver contraptions, read a card at the end of it, and produce a short blade. The boy meanwhile, also with blade, approached the nearest spectator, inert, grabbed the hair—long long hair, thought Rick, long hair of a girl— and tossed her head back so that her chest was uppermost.

With speed he slashed her blouse, knife a blur, stabbed and cut, carried a heart to the silvery framework. The girl lay back, a vacant expression on her face, one breast awkwardly hanging from the side of the wound in her chest.

The golden girl and boy darted back and forth, working with

feverish speed, organs, legs, fingers, eyes, blood flowing in a dreamy blur.

Rick lost track of the detail, and did not notice when he contributed a foot, a left arm from the elbow down, and a kidney.

He dimly saw a stream of silver frames being wheeled in, the two dervishes noting cards and whirling to bodies, and back again laden with new fruits. In came the frames, and out again. In and out.

Then he was aware of a pause. The last silver—trolley?—had been wheeled out.

But again the creatures moved into a blur, darting hither and thither amongst Rick and his disorganized villagers, dragging this one to that, sewing here, cutting again there. He lost consciousness, finally, as his head and shoulders, and ribcage, were attached to the waist of some blood-smeared girl.

A tithe of the villagers awoke in new circumstances next day, the agonies and adjustments provoking much comment in the area.

Despite the passing of the seasons, Baron de Quincy's original Healing Orgy was not seen there again, though talk sometimes drifted in of the famous and wealthy surviving unpredictable accidents and diseases.

David Grigg

Crippled Spinner

The machine wove a web of silver against the stars, binding Cassiopeia, Orion, and blazing Sirius in a delicate trap.

Ariane looked on the work of the Spinner, her mechanical spider, and smiled. She sat in a tight bubble, insulated against the void, warm and safe. She felt good, creative, making something beautiful and at the same time practical. A womanly task, she thought. She smiled again, this time at the image of herself at an ancient spinning wheel, creating thread. Thread from which sails would be woven.

When this part of the web was done, Marc would move in and fill in the strands with micro-thin weave. Blocking out the view of the stars, she thought, and made a sad face.

"How goes it?" said Marc, from many miles away. The radio wave took a full minute to reach her from where Marc was. "The third quadrant's almost done," she said, and adjusted controls to tighten the work of the Spinner as she waited for his reply. It was a strange feeling, being here in the bubble in the midst of space. If she did not turn, to see the bulk of her ship behind her, she could imagine herself floating alone, without support in the endless womb of space. The machine went on weaving.

Sometimes Ariane felt like driving the Spinner to her own whim, creating fantastic abstract designs against the velvet backdrop of stars. But that would be without a practical use: a wrong thing. Still, it was nice to dream.

"That's great!" Marc's voice, back again. "I've started filling in the sail on the second quadrant. We'll have to be careful from now on: the light pressure's already starting to push the sail we've got. The faster we finish the better. John says the pod has left Earth already. Should be here in just a few days."

She made no reply: stretched out conversations generally destroyed the trivia of speech.

Alone in space. Floating in the delicious void, swimming like a newborn fish in a dark and open sea. And in front of her was a net of silver, waiting to grasp her and haul her above an unseen, unknowable surface.

Ariane reached to touch the soft plastic bubble before her face, to reassure herself of its reality. Sometimes her mind seemed to go journeying on its own, beyond her control.

The web now trapped the Pleiades: they sparkled, brilliant sisters, jewels amidst the bright hair of the web.

Behind her ship was the blazing sun, blowing outwards, gusting forth a wind between the stars. A wind they planned to sail.

The shining spider wove on. Ariane, idly dreaming, neglected her instruments in the control device she held. Out in space, in one small square of the web, a streaming comet lay, its ghostly tresses tossed back by the eternal wind from the sun.

There was a red light on the control.

It was a long time before she noticed it, before she could bring her mind back from the stars. A red light. It was as though her mind could not focus. Meteor warning—that was it. Meteors. She moved quickly, then, and switched on her ship defensive shield. Immediately, the stars were filtered through a rosy shimmer: they danced like red sparks.

But before she could take any further action, two more red lights came on. The Spinner had been hit. The damage—she could not tell as yet. She bit her lip, feeling frustration. The meteor warning light stayed on, and she waited long tense minutes for the shower to pass. At last, the warning light went out, a red eye closing, and she snapped off the ruddy shield. Again the stars stood out clear and white. She searched for the Spinner with her eyes.

It was coming toward her.

She could see loose mechanisms spilling out like entrails from its smashed interior. And behind it raced the wire, the silver wire. She was paralysed. The Spinner rushed up at her, loomed huge and menacing, and then was past. Ariane sat very still, wide-eyed, seeing the wire stream past like an endless ticker-tape. She knew, intellectually, that the Spinner had missed her by hundreds of feet, but knowing was not feeling, and she shook with fear. And the web!

The web was unwinding.

Strand by strand, it came apart. Ariane was immobilized by horror, watching the unravelling miles of wire.

She turned her ship, at last, to follow the crippled Spinner. There was the babble of Marc's voice in her ears, but she could not listen.

The Spinner was crazy. It was like a spider crazed by an hallucinogen, a manic weaver. It moved and spun as it should, but erratically; it made knots and patterns like a schizophrenic. And pulled strands across the rest of the completed sail. She could see the Spinner and its tangled web black now against the white sail, flexing it and pulling it along.

"Destruct, Ariane!" came Marc's voice. But she did not hear. Her mind had been snared by the harmony and magic in the random silver lines, by something hypnotic in the amazing network of gleaming wire.

Loops of the web spun around her ship: a thick rope wrapped around her bubble, and she saw the fine structure of it as if for the first time; the micro-strands that made the cord, the cords braided to make the rope. She had never seen the wire so close before.

Then the bubble jerked suddenly, and she was thrown against the plastic surface. Again, and the ship swung, so that she could see the huge mass of the sail, and the wire that bound her to it. She could see, far off, the tugs which held the sail in place while it was being constructed: they too seemed looped with the endless thread. Like Christmas ribbon, she thought detachedly: how beautiful it seems!

The tugs had released the sail, that was it. And the Spinner, the crippled, crazy Spinner, had at last died, ran out of wire.

The sail billowed slowly, very slowly, above her, like that of a great sailing ship. And she swung below, a tiny ship beneath a vast sail.

The tugs were fouled in the wire, she could see them clearly, unable to move amidst the knots of the mad web.

There was only the gentlest of accelerations on Ariane, the softest of reminders as the sail filled with the wind from the sun and started out with her as cargo on its long voyage between the stars.

Kathryn Buckley and Rob Gerrand

Pegasus

Being an explication and exegisis of the
brain-patterns of the science-fiction author.

Illusion and fission
and far-reaching vision
converging and merging
in perfect precision.

Mystical twists
statistical lists
arranging ideas
of greeblies and seers
round atmospheres
clanging of gears
noses and ears
graft and corruption
dust of destruction
trees that are crumbling
dwarves that are grumbling
crabs that are fumbling
roots ornamental
stones monumental
whirling and
swirling
giggling and

gurgling
planets emerging
timelines diverging
gadgets and robots
computers and new lots
of android and alien
who battle and fail in
their contests with man
growth ecologic
spacewarps spasmodic
dreams episodic
brains positronic
sorcerers demonic
chthonic
moronic
end-of-world plans
disasters pernicious
commanders suspicious
space-cubs naive
scientists didactic
maidens pneumatic
all fit quite pragmatic
you have to believe

It's coincidental
and quite accidental
ideas that we use
have a very short fuse
and serve to confuse
all those who refuse
to follow the same
unexpected and strange
mind-bending range
of thoughts that we do

The fans understand us
the world cannot stand us
no use reprimand us

you cannot demand us
to give in
and live in
a sieve in
which ideas like treacle
would dribble and trickle
and trickle
no more

No mor-
tal should chor-
tle at all our contor-
ting of por-
tals of time
and dispor-
tings sublime

If you are content
with the world just a tent
we'll invent an event
we'll rent you a rent
in the fabric of time
and the life you have spent
which will make you relent
AND
THEN
YOU'LL
BE
MINE!!!!!!!!!!

Ursula K. Le Guin

The Eye Altering (II)

Miriam stood at the big window of the infirmary ward and looked out at the view and thought, For twenty-five years I have been standing at this window and looking out at this view. And never once have I seen what I wanted to see.

If I forget thee, O Jerusalem—

The pain was forgotten, yes. The hatred and the fear, forgotten. In exile you don't remember the gray days and the black years. You remember the sunlight, the orchards, the white cities. Even when you try to forget it you remember that Jerusalem was golden.

The sky outside the ward window was dulled with haze. Over the low ridge called Ararat the sun was setting; setting slowly, for New Zion had a slower spin than Old Earth, and a twenty-eight hour day; settling, rather than setting—settling dully down onto the dull horizon. There were no clouds to gather the colors of sunset. There were seldom any clouds. When the haze thickened it rained, a misty, smothering rain; when the haze was thin, as now, it hung high and vague, formless. It never quite cleared. You never saw the color of the sky. You never saw the stars. And through the haze the sun, no, not the sun, but NSC 641 (Class G) burned swollen and vaporous, warty as an orange—remember oranges? the sweet juice on the tongue? the orchards of Haifa?—NSC 641 stared, like a bleary eye. And you could stare back at it. No glory of gold to blind you. Two imbeciles staring at each other.

Shadows stretched across the valley toward the buildings of the Settlement. In shadow the fields and woods were black; in the light they were brown, purplish, and dark red. Dirty colors, the colors you got when you scrubbed your watercolors too much and the teacher came by and said, You'd better use some fresh water, Mimi, it's getting muddy. Because the teacher had been too kind to say to a ten-year-old, That picture's a total loss, Mimi, throw it away and start fresh.

She had thought of that before—she had thought all her thoughts before, standing at this window—but this time it reminded her of Genya, because of the painting, and she turned to see how he was doing. The shock symptoms were almost gone, his face was no longer so pale and his pulse had steadied. While she held his wrist he sighed a bit and opened his eyes. Lovely eyes he had, gray in the thin face. He had never been much but eyes, poor Genya. Her oldest patient. Twenty-four years he had been her patient, right from the moment of his birth, five pounds, purplish-blue like a fetal rat, a month premature and half dead of cyanosis: the fifth child born on New Zion, the first in Ararat Settlement. A native. A feeble and unpromising native. He hadn't even had the strength, or the sense, to cry at his first breath of this alien air. Sofia's other children had been full term and healthy, two girls, both married and mothers now, and fat Leon who could hoist a seventy-kilo sack of grain when he was fifteen. Good young colonists, strong stock. But Miriam had always loved Genya, and all the more after her own years of miscarriages and stillbirths, and the last birth, the girl who had lived two hours, whose eyes had been clear gray like Genya's. Babies never have gray eyes, the eyes of the newborn are blue, that was all sentimental rubbish. But how could you ever make sure of what color things were under this damned warty-orange sun? Nothing ever looked right. "So there you are, Gennady Borisovich," she said, "back home, eh?"

It had been their joke when he was a child; he had spent so much time in the infirmary that whenever he came in with one of his fevers or fainting-spells or gasping asthma he would say, "Here I am, back home, Auntie Doctor...."

"What happened?" he asked.

"You collapsed. Hoeing down in the South Field. Aaron and Tina brought you up here on the tractor. Touch of sunstroke, maybe? You've been doing all right, haven't you?"

He shrugged and nodded.

"Dizzy? Short of breath?"

"On and off."

"Why didn't you come to the clinic?"

"It's no good, Miriam."

Since he was grown he had called her Miriam. She missed "Auntie Doctor." He had grown away from her, these last few years, withdrawn from her into his painting. He had always sketched and painted, but now, all his free time and whatever energy he had left when his Settlement duties were done, he spent in the loft of the generator building where he'd made a kind of studio, grinding colors from rocks and mixing dyes from native plants, making brushes by begging pigtail-ends off little girls, and painting—painting on scraps from the lumbermill, on bits of rag, on precious scraps of paper, on smooth slabs of slate from the quarry on Ararat if nothing better was at hand. Painting portraits, scenes of Settlement life, buildings, machinery, still-lifes, plants, landscapes, inner visions. Painting anything, everything. His portraits had been much in demand— people were always kind to Genya and the other sicklies—but lately he had not done any portraits; he had gone in for queer muddy jumbles of forms and lines all in a dark haze, like worlds half-created. Nobody liked those paintings, but nobody ever told Genya he was wasting his time. He was a sickly; he was an artist; OK. Healthy people had no time to be artists. There was too much work to do. But it was good to have an artist. It was human. It was like Earth. Wasn't it?

They were kind to Toby, too, whose stomach troubles were so bad that at sixteen he weighed eighty-four pounds; kind to little Shura, who was just learning to talk at six, and whose eyes wept and wept all day long, even when she was smiling; kind to all their sicklies, the ones whose bodies could not adjust to this alien world, whose stomachs could not digest the native proteins even with the help of the metas, the metabolizing pills which every colonist must take twice a day every day of his life on New Zion. Hard as life was in the Twenty Settlements, much as they needed every hand to work, they were gentle with their useless ones, their afflicted. In affliction the hand of God is visible. They remembered the words civilization, humanity. They remembered Jerusalem.

"Genya, my dear, what do you mean, it's no good?"

His quiet voice had frightened her. "It's no good," he had said, smiling. And the gray eyes not clear but veiled, hazy.

"Medicine," he said. "Pills. Cures."

"Of course you know more about medicine than I do," Miriam said. "You're a much better doctor than I am. Or are you giving up? Is that it, Genya? Giving up?" Anger had come upon her so suddenly, from so deep within, from anxiety so long and deeply hidden, that it shook her body and cracked her voice.

"I'm giving up one thing. The metas."

"Metas? Giving them up? What are you talking about?"

"I haven't taken any for two weeks."

The despairing rage swelled in her; she felt her face go hot, so that it felt twice its normal size—"Two weeks! And so, and so, and so you're here! Where did you think you'd end up, you terrible fool? Lucky you're not dead!"

"I haven't been any worse since I stopped taking them, Miriam. Better, this whole last week. Until today. It can't be that. It must have been heatstroke. I—forgot to wear a hat. . . ." He too flushed faintly, in the eagerness of his pleading, or with shame. It was stupid to work in the fields bareheaded; for all its dull look NSC 641 could hit the unsheltered human head quite as hard as fiery Sol, and Genya was apologetic for his carelessness. "You see, I was feeling fine this morning, really good, I kept right up with the others hoeing. Then I felt a bit dizzy, but I didn't want to stop, it was so good to be able to work right with the others, I never thought about heatstroke."

Miriam found that there were tears in her eyes, and this made her so ultimately and absolutely angry that she couldn't speak at all. She got up off Genya's bed and strode off down the ward between the rows of beds, four on one side, four on the other. She strode back and stood staring out the window at the mud-colored shapeless ugly world.

Genya was saying something—"Miriam, honestly, couldn't it be that the metas are worse for me than the native proteins are?"—but she did not listen; the grief and wrath and fear swelled in her and swelled in her, and broke, and she cried out, "O Genya, Genya, how could you? Not you, to give up now, after fighting so long—I can't bear it! I can't bear it!" But she did not cry it out aloud. Not one word of it. Never. She cried out in her mind, and some tears came out and ran down her cheeks, but her back was turned to the patient. She looked through distorting tears at the flat valley and the dull sun and said to them a silent, "I hate you." Then after a while she could turn around and say aloud, "Lie down,"—for he had sat up, distressed by her long silence—"lie down, be quiet. You'll take two metas before dinner. If you need anything, Geza's in the nurse's station." And she walked out.

As she left the infirmary she saw Tina climbing up the back path from the fields, coming to see how Genya was, no doubt. For all his wheezes and fevers Genya had never wanted for girlfriends. Tina, and Shoshanna, and Bella, and Rachel, he could have had his pick. But last year when he and Rachel were living together, they had got contraceptives from the clinic regularly, and then they had separated; they hadn't married, though by his age, twenty-four, all Settlement kids were married and parents. He hadn't married Rachel, and Miriam knew why. Moral genetics. Bad genes. Sickly genes. Shouldn't pass them on to the next generation. Weed out the sicklies. No procreation for him, and therefore no marriage; he couldn't ask Rachel to live barren for the love of him. What the Settlements needed was children, plenty of healthy young natives who, with the help of the meta pills, could survive on this planet.

Rachel hadn't taken up with anybody else. But she was only eighteen. She'd get over it. Marry a boy from another Settlement, most likely, and move away, away from Genya's big gray eyes. It would be best for her. And for him.

No wonder Genya was suicidal! Miriam thought, and put the thought away from her fiercely, wearily. She was very weary. She had meant to go to her room and wash, change her clothes, change her mood, before dinner; but the room was so lonesome with Leonid away at Salem Settlement and not due back for at least another month, she couldn't stand it. She went straight across the dusty central square of the Settlement to the refectory building, and into the Living Room. To get away, clear away, from the windless haze and the gray sky and the ugly sun.

Nobody was in the Living Room but Commander Marca, fast asleep on one of the padded wooden couches, and Reine, reading. The two oldest members of the Settlement. Commander Marca was in fact the oldest person in the world. He had been forty-four when he piloted the Exile Fleet from Old Earth to New Zion; he was seventy now, and very frail. People didn't wear well here. They aged early, died at fifty, sixty. Reine, the biochemist, was forty-five now but looked twenty years older. It's a damned geriatric club, Miriam thought sourly; and it was true that the young, the Zionborn, seldom used the Living Room. They came there to read, as it held the Settlement's library of books and tapes and microfilm, but not many of them read much, or had much time to read. And maybe the April light and the pictures made them a little uneasy. They were such moral, severe, serious young people; there was no leisure in their lives, no beauty in their world; how could they approve of this luxury their elders needed, this one haven, this one place like home....

The Living Room had no windows. Avram, a wizard with anything electrical, had done the indirect lighting, deliberately reproducing the color and quality of sunlight—not NSC 641 light, but sunlight—so that to enter the Living Room was to enter a room in a house on Earth on a warm sunny day of April or early May, to see all things in that clear, clean, lovely light. Avram and several others had worked on the pictures, enlarging colored photos to a meter or so square: scenes of Earth, photographs and paintings brought by the colonists—Venice, the Negev, the domes of the Kremlin, a farm in Portugal, the Dead Sea, Hampstead Heath, a beach in Oregon, a meadow in Poland, cities, forests, mountains, Van Gogh's cypresses, Bierstadt's Rocky Mountains, Monet's waterlilies, Leonardo's blue mysterious caves. Every wall of the room was covered with pictures, dozens of pictures, all the beauty of the Earth. So that the Earthborn could see and remember, so that the Zionborn could see and know.

There had been some discussion about the pictures, twenty years ago when Avram had started putting them up: Was it really wise? Should we look back? And so on. But then Commander Marca had come by on a visit, seen the Living Room of Ararat Settlement, and said, "This is where I'll stay." With every Settlement vying to have him, he had chosen Ararat. Because of the pictures of Earth, because of the light of Earth in that room, shining on the green fields, the snowy peaks, the golden forests of autumn, the flights of gulls above the sea, the white and red and rose of waterlilies on blue pools—clear colors, true, pure, the colors of the Earth.

He slept there now, a handsome old man. Outside, in the hard, dull, orange daylight, he would look sick and old, his cheeks veined and muddy. Here you could see what he looked like.

Miriam sat down near him, facing her favorite picture, a quiet landscape by Corot, trees over a silvery stream. She was so tired that for once she was willing to just sit, in a mild stupor. Through the stupor, faintly, idly, words came floating. Couldn't it be . . . Honestly, couldn't it be that the metas are worse . . . Miriam, honestly, couldn't it be . . .

"Do you think I never thought of that?" she retorted in silence. "Idiot! Do you think I don't know the metas are hard on your guts? Didn't I try fifty different combinations while you were a kid, trying to get rid of the side effects? But it's not as bad as being allergic to the whole damn planet, and that's what we all are! If we don't take the metas just as a diabetic takes insulin, we starve. Our bodies aren't built to handle Zion proteins. We get sick, cramps, diarrhoea, convulsions, and starve. You know better than the doctor, do you? Don't give me that. You're trying to—" But she broke off the silent dialogue abruptly. Genya was not trying to kill himself. He was not. He would not. He had courage, that one. And brains.

"All right," she said to the quiet young man in her mind. "All right! If you'll stay in the infirmary, under observation—for two weeks, and do exactly what I say—all right, I'll try it!"

Because, said another, even quieter voice deep in her, it doesn't really matter. Whatever you do or don't do, he will die. This year; next year. Two hours; twenty-four years. The sicklies can't adjust to this world. And neither can we, neither can we. We weren't meant to live here, Genya my dear. We weren't made for this world, nor it for us. We were made of earth, by earth, to live on earth, under the blue sky and the golden sun.

The dinner gong began to ring. Going into the refectory she met little Shura. The child carried a bunch of the repulsive blackish-purple native weeds, as a child at home would carry a bunch of white daisies, red poppies picked in the fields. Shura's eyes were teary as usual, but she smiled up at Auntie Doctor. Her lips looked pallid in the red-orange light of sunset through the windows. Everybody's lips looked pallid. Everybody's face looked tired, set, stoical, after the long day's work, as they went into the Settlement dining hall, all together, the three hundred exiles of Ararat on Zion, the eleventh lost tribe.

*   *   *

He was doing very well. She had to admit it. "You're doing well," she said, and he, with his grin, "I told you so!"

"It could be because you're not doing anything else," she said, "smart ass."

"Not doing anything? I filed health records for Geza all morning, I played games with Rosie and Moishe for two hours, I've been grinding colors all afternoon—say, I need more mineral oil, can I have another litre? It's a much better pigment vehicle than the vegetable oil."

"Sure. But listen, I have something for you better than that. Little Tel Aviv has got their pulp mill going full time. They sent a truck over yesterday with paper—"

"Paper?"

"Half a ton of it! I took two hundred sheets for you. It's in the office." He was off like a shot, and was into the bundle of paper before she even got there. "Oh, God," he said, holding up a sheet, "beautiful, it's beautiful!" And she thought how often she had heard him say that, "Beautiful!" of one drab useful thing or another. He didn't know what beauty was; he'd never seen any. The paper was thick, substantial, grayish, in big sheets, intended to be cut small and used sparingly, of course; but let him have it for his painting. There was little enough else she could give him.

"When you let me out of here," Genya said, hugging the unwieldy bundle with both arms, "I'll go over to Tel Aviv and paint their pulp mill, I'll immortalize their pulp mill!"

"You'd better go lie down."

"No, listen, I promised Moishe I'd beat him at chess. What's wrong with him, anyhow?"

"Rashes, edema."

"He's like me?"

Miriam shrugged. "He was fine till this year. Puberty triggered something. Not unusual with allergic symptoms."

"What is allergy, anyhow?"

"Well, call it a failure of adaptation. Back home, people used to feed babies cows' milk, from bottles. Some of the babies could adapt to it, but some got rashes, breathing trouble, colic. The cow's key didn't fit their metabolic lock. Well, New Zion's protein keys don't fit our locks; so we have to change our metabolism with the metas."

"Would Moishe or I have been an allergic on Earth?"

"I don't know. You might; prematures often are. Irving, he died, oh, twenty years ago, he was allergic to this terrible list of things on Earth, they should never have let him come, poor thing, he spends his life on Earth half-suffocated and comes here and starves to death even on a quadruple dose of metas."

"Aha," said Genya, "you shouldn't have given him metas at all. Just Zion mush."

"Zion mush?" Only one of the native grains yielded enough to be worth harvesting, and it produced a gluey meal which could not be baked.

"I ate three bowls of it for lunch."

"He lies around the hospital all day complaining," Miriam said, "and then stuffs his belly with that slop. How can an artistic soul eat something that tastes like jellied bilge?"

"You feed it to your helpless child patients in your own hospital! I just ate the leftovers."

"Oh, get along with you."

"I am. I want to paint while the sun's still up. On a piece of new paper, a whole piece of new paper...."

It had been a long day at the clinic, but there were no in-patients. She had sent Osip home last night in a cast with a good scolding for being so careless as to tip his tractor over, endangering not only his life but the tractor, which was even harder to replace. And young Moishe had gone back to the children's house, though she didn't like the way his rash kept coming back. And Rosie was over her asthma, and the Commander's heart was doing as well as could be expected; so the ward was empty, except for her permanent inmate of the past two weeks, Genya.

He was sprawled out on his bed under the window, so lax and still that she had a moment of alarm; but his color was good, he breathed evenly, he was simply asleep, deeply asleep, the way people slept after a hard day in the fields, exhausted.

He had been painting. He had cleaned up the rags and brushes; he always cleaned up promptly and thoroughly, but the picture stood on his makeshift easel. Usually these days he was secretive about his paintings, hid them, since people had stopped admiring them. The

Commander had murmured to her, "What ugly stuff, poor boy!" But she had heard young Moishe, watching Genya paint, say, "How do you do it, Genya, how do you make it so pretty?" and Genya answer, "Beauty's in the eye, Moishe."

Well, that was true, and she went closer to look at the painting in the dull afternoon light. Genya had painted the view out the big window of the ward. Nothing vague and half-created this time: realistic, all too realistic. Hideously recognizable. There was the flat ridge of Ararat, the mud-colored trees and fields, the hazy sky, the storage barn and a corner of the school building in the foreground. Her eyes went from the painted scene to the real one. To spend hours, days, painting that! What a waste, what a waste.

It was hard on Genya, it was sad, the way he hid his paintings now, knowing that nobody would want to see them, except maybe a child like Moishe fascinated with the mere skill of the hand, the craftsman's dexterity.

That night as Genya helped her straighten up the injection cabinets—he was a good deal of help around the infirmary these days—she said, "I like the picture you painted today."

"I finished it today," he corrected her. "Damn thing took all week. I'm just beginning to learn to see."

"Can I put it up in the Living Room?"

He looked at her across a tray of hypodermic needles, his eyes quiet and a little quizzical. "In the Living Room? But that's all pictures of Home."

"It's time maybe we had some pictures of our new home there."

"A moral gesture, eh? Sure, OK. If you like it."

"I like it very much," she lied blandly.

"It isn't bad," he said. "I'll do better, though, when I've learned how to fit myself to the pattern."

"What pattern?"

"Well, you know, you have to look until you *see* the pattern, till it makes sense, and then you have to get that into your hand, too." He made large, vague, shaping gestures with a bottle of absolute alcohol.

"Anybody who asks a painter a question in words deserves what they get, I guess," said Miriam. "Babble, babble. You take the picture over tomorrow and put it up. Artists are so temperamental about where they get their pictures hung, and the lighting and everything.

Besides, it's time you were getting out. A little. An hour or two a day. No more."

"Can I eat dinner in the dining hall, then?"

"All right. It'll keep Tina from coming here to keep you from being lonely and eating up all the infirmary rations. That girl eats like a vacuum pump. Listen, if you go out in the middle of the day, will you kindly take the trouble to wear a hat?"

"You think I'm right, then."

"Right?"

"That it was sunstroke."

"That was *my* diagnosis, if you will recall."

"All right: but my addition was that I do better without metas."

"I have no idea. You've got along fine before for weeks, and then poof, down again. Nothing whatever has been proved."

"But a pattern has been established! I've lived a month without metas, and gained six pounds."

"And edema of the head, Mr. Know-It-All?"

She saw him the next day sitting with Rachel, just before dinner time, on the slope below the storage barn. Rachel had not come to see him in the infirmary. They sat side by side, very close together, motionless, not talking.

Miriam went on to the Living Room. A half hour there before dinner had become a habit with her lately. It seemed to rest her from the weariness of the day. But the room was less peaceful than usual this evening; the Commander was awake, and talking with Reine and Avram. "Well, where did it come from then?" he was saying in his heavy Italian accent—he had not learned Hebrew till he was forty, in the Transit Camp. "Who put it there?" Then seeing Miriam he greeted her as always with a grand cordiality of voice and gesture. "Ah, Doctor! Please, join us, come, solve our mystery for us. You know each picture in this room as well as I do. Where, do you think, and when did we acquire the new one? You see?"

"It's Genya's," Miriam was about to say, when she saw the new picture. It wasn't Genya's. It was a painting, all right, and a landscape, but a landscape of the Earth: a wide valley, the fields green and green-gold, orchards coming into flower, the sweeping slope of a mountain in the distance, a tower, perhaps a castle or medieval farm-building, in the foreground, and over all the pure, subtle, sunlit sky. It was a complex and happy painting, a celebration of the spring, an act of praise.

"How beautiful," she said, her voice catching. "Didn't you put it up, Avram?"

"Me? I can photograph, I can't paint. Look at it, it's no reproduction. Some kind of tempera or oils, see?"

"Somebody brought it from Home. Had it in their baggage," Reine suggested.

"For twenty-five years?" said the Commander. "Why? And who? We all know what all the others have!"

"No. I think," Miriam was confused, and stammered, "I think it's something Genya did. I asked him to put up one of his paintings here. Not this one. How did he do this?"

"Copied from a photograph," Avram suggested.

"No no no no, impossible," old Marca said, outraged. "That is a painting, not a copy! That is a work of art, that was seen, seen with the eyes and the heart!"

With the eyes and the heart.

Miriam looked, and she saw. She saw what the light of NSC 641 had hidden from her, what the artificial Earth daylight of the room revealed to her. She saw what Genya saw: the beauty of the world.

"I think it must be in Central France, the Auvergne," Reine was saying wistfully, and the Commander, "O no no no, it's near Lake Como, I am certain," and Avram, "Well it looks to me like where I grew up in the Caucasus," when they all turned to look at Miriam. She had made a strange noise, a gasp or laugh or sob. "It's here," she said. "Here. That's Ararat. The mountain. That's the fields, our fields, our trees. That's the corner of the school, that tower. See it? It's here. Zion. It's how Genya sees it. With the eyes and the heart."

"But look, the trees are green, look at the colors, Miriam. It's Earth—"

"Yes! It is Earth. Genya's Earth!"

"But he can't—"

"How do we know? How do we know what a child of Zion sees? We can see the picture in this light that's like Home. Take it outside, into the daylight, and you'll see what we always see, the ugly colors, the ugly planet where we're not at home. But he is at home! He is! It's we," Miriam said, laughing in tears, looking at them all, the anxious, tired, elderly faces, "*we* who lack the key. We with our—with our—" she stumbled and leapt at the idea like a horse at a high wall, "with our meta pills!"

They all stared at her.

"With our meta pills, we can survive here, just barely, right? But don't you see, he *lives* here! We were all perfectly adjusted to Earth, too well, we can't fit anywhere else—he wasn't, wouldn't have been; allergic, a misfit—the pattern a little wrong, see? The pattern. But there are many patterns, infinite patterns, he fits this one a little better than we do—"

Avram and the Commander continued to stare. Reine shot an alarmed glance at the picture, but asked gamely, "You're saying that Genya's allergies—"

"Not just Genya! All the sicklies, maybe! For twenty-five years I've been feeding them metas, and they're allergic to *Earth* proteins, the metas just foul them up, they're a different pattern, oh idiot! Idiot! Oh, my God, he and Rachel can get married. They've got to marry, he should have kids. What about Rachel taking metas while she's pregnant, the fetus. I can work it out, I can work it out. I must call Leonid. And Moishe, thank God! maybe he's another one! Listen, I must go talk to Genya and Rachel, immediately. Excuse me!" She left, a short, gray woman moving like a lightning bolt.

Marca, Avram, and Reine stood staring after her, at each other, and finally back at Genya's painting.

It hung there before them, serene and joyful, full of light.

"I don't understand," said Avram.

"Patterns," Reine said thoughtfully.

"It is very beautiful," said the old Commander of the Exile Fleet. "Only, it makes me homesick."

I can't imagine myself ever rereading Heinlein's The Moon Is A Harsh Mistress *without feeling a wistful pang of loss. I think it was Ursula who said, toward the end of the workshop, that "The group marriage is dissolving; the members of the newly-formed family parting, perhaps never to meet again together in the same place or at the same time." But it might have been any one of us; the feeling was pervasive.*

Some time after the workshop, I attended a "seminar" for writers in Tasmania. Olaf Ruhen was the "speaker": he took up a position in front of his "audience" and talked . . . and talked . . . and talked, while everyone scribbled notes furiously. A Clarion-style workshop it was not. No wonder my mind began wandering back to Booth Lodge.

I remember Ursula, along with the rest of us, discussing her trunkful of unfinished stories that start off real good, but which she somehow never managed to finish. Randal Flynn, reading out a story about Egbert the Grong, in a style reminiscent of David Hemmings narrating the text of Rick Wakeman's "Journey to the Center of the Earth" album. Ursula and Kitty discussing their cats . . .

But the day after I returned to Tasmania I was back at my old job. My workmates appear to have only two major interests in their lives: sex and excrement; their conversation over the past year could be easily condensed on to a single sheet of toilet paper. One morning, during tea-break, one of them caught me reading the Star Trek Fleet Manual, *and asked if he could have a look at it. In less than fifteen seconds he had located a dirty picture. Now, with the* Star Fleet Manual, *this isn't easy—but he managed. If you have one of these publications, and if you are interested, then the "dirty" picture can be found on pages T0: 01: 03: 12 and 14. But you'll have to look real close.*

Yes, the workshop is over and I'm home again. At night I can look up and see the silver haze of the Milky Way edge-on. Somewhere out there, lost in immensity and eternity, there has to be other planets and life forms and cultures as yet undreamed of. But the sky is also . . . the sky. The stars are only decorations. And anyone who spends too much time staring at them must be a little crazy. So tomorrow I resume my job in order to eat, so that I may resume my job . . .

Welcome back to the Real World.

BRUCE BARNES